PITCHING

JIM PALMER

Pitching

EDITED BY **JOEL H. COHEN**

ATHENEUM 1975 NEW YORK

Photographs by TADDER / Baltimore

COPYRIGHT © 1975 BY JIM PALMER AND JOEL H. COHEN
ALL RIGHTS RESERVED
LIBRARY OF CONGRESS CATALOG CARD NUMBER 74–77855
ISBN 0–689–10627–0
PUBLISHED SIMULTANEOUSLY IN CANADA BY MC CLELLAND
AND STEWART LTD.
COMPOSITION BY CONNECTICUT PRINTERS, INC., HARTFORD, CONNECTICUT
PRINTED AND BOUND BY THE BOOK PRESS, BRATTLEBORO, VERMONT
DESIGNED BY KATHLEEN CAREY
FIRST EDITION

MY THANKS TO SO MANY FOR MAKING

A BOY'S DREAM A MAN'S REALITY

Contents

THE FUN OF PITCHING   3

DECIDING TO BE A PITCHER   6

EQUIPMENT AND OTHER AIDS   17

DELIVERY   47

THROWING THE PITCHES   88

CONTROL   110

CONDITIONING   135

STRATEGY IN PITCHING   153

DEFENSE   178

THE PSYCHOLOGY OF PITCHING   197

PITCHING

The Fun of Pitching

WHETHER IT'S baseball, golf, tennis, or basketball, I enjoy being athletically involved.

So, while baseball has provided me with a very successful career, I don't think of it so much as a job but as a joy.

Pitching is particularly enjoyable because of the key role the pitcher plays in the outcome of the game. If you're highly competitive, pitching is excellent because in high school and even on the college level it gives you the chance to almost personally determine your fate and that of your ball club.

I say *almost,* because I don't mean to minimize the importance of the club behind you. For any pitcher to win games, his teammates have to score runs and play good defense. Very few pitchers, if any, in major-league baseball—possibly Tom Seaver, Bob Gibson, Steve Carlton and Nolan Ryan—can go to the mound on a given day and win or lose a ball game themselves. It takes an

3

overpowering pitcher who can strike out a lot of men to offset what happens behind him. But overpowering or not, the pitcher is the main man—the fellow on the firing line whose performance will result in a good day or bad day for his team. Accordingly, he's the matador, the orchestra leader, the tightrope walker, the man the spotlight is on.

Of course, being so much in control of events is a mixed blessing. It's one of the good things about being a pitcher, but also one of the bad. There are times when the pressure becomes a tremendous burden. I remember when I pitched the opening game of the 1970 World Series, feeling intensely that twenty-four men were relying on me. When I gave up three runs early in the game, I felt I'd let the ball club down. But then I shut them out for seven innings and we won, 4–3—and believe me, the satisfaction more than made up for the pressure.

Whether you already are a pitcher, or you're considering becoming one—or even if you just want to get a better appreciation of baseball from the pitcher's point of view—I hope the experiences and observations that are set down in this book will help you.* As you read, though, keep in mind that there are more ways than one to do things—your coach or manager knows you personally and his advice should come first—and some things that apply to major-league pitching are a little too advanced for you right now. And remember that even the best theories aren't going to help until you put them into practice.

*Incidentally, I've written this book from the viewpoint of a right-handed pitcher. If you're a lefty, just reverse things—change right foot to left foot, and so on—where appropriate. The general principles of pitching, of course, apply equally whichever hand you use to pitch.

Pitching is hard and demanding work. It requires stamina, brains, courage, and special ability, natural or developed, but when it's well done, there are few things more satisfying in the world of sports. Let's talk about how to make sure you do *your* pitching as skillfully as you possibly can, and thus with as much pleasure as the game can offer.

Sincerely,
JIM PALMER

Deciding to Be a Pitcher

S H O U L D Y O U be a pitcher? How do you decide whether the mound or another position is the best place for you?

The main consideration should be how well you do at pitching, compared with your other baseball skills. Another factor is your natural throwing ability.

When I was a youngster I could run fast enough and hit well enough to play the field, but I could pitch a little bit better. I had what's referred to as a "good arm," another way of saying the natural ability to throw the fast ball. Many baseball experts believe that a young player cannot be taught to throw the fast ball, so they look for players who can. When a scout sees a boy who has an outstanding arm, who can throw the ball hard, he figures that boy can be taught to throw the curve, slider, and change-up. The strength of the arm is the important quality.

Another way to look at the situation is to judge how

well you do in other facets of the game. If you can hit, run, throw and field, it would probably be better for you to become an infielder or outfielder. If you can't do those things particularly well, it's probably better to work at becoming a pitcher—providing you've got a strong enough arm.

You'll find that often the best athletes on Little League or high school baseball teams are pitchers. On the days they don't pitch, they play in the field. Very few young pitchers are just pitchers.

When I was on the team at Scottsdale High School in Arizona, I played every position. We were in the state tournament one year and our shortstop broke his ankle, so I ended up at short. I did a good enough job to get by. But most of all, I enjoyed playing the outfield. I didn't particularly care where, but it was usually center field. I had a good arm and I enjoyed throwing runners out.

In Little League in California, where we moved from Westchester County in New York, I started out as a third baseman. I must have been a defensive star, because they kept me in the lineup even though I was hitting only .160. I also pitched a game and won it, 1–0, so it looked as though I had a future on the mound. I really pitched so much better and threw so much harder than most kids my age, I was later chosen to be a pitcher.

Actually, despite that .160 batting average, my hitting was good through high school. I hit about .480 every year until I was a senior. Then I developed an eye problem, an astigmatism, and wound up hitting about .330. That's not a bad batting average, but far below what I'd hit the two years before. The eye doctor's discovery of that astigmatism in my left eye convinced me that I belonged on the mound. Few good hitters wear glasses, something I would have tried if I hadn't become a pitcher.

The decision was finalized when I went to South Dakota, still a high school student, to play with college athletes in the Basin League. I went there as a pitcher-outfielder, and I made the mistake (if you want to call it that) of throwing before I got a chance to hit, and they decided right there that I would be a pitcher.

The only regrets I've had (aside from being knocked out of the box) was that playing another position would enable me to participate in 150 or 160 games a year, rather than endure the boredom of sitting out three of every four ball games.

But pitching is a good life. Being out of so many games, you have a chance to watch the strategic moves of different managers, not only your own, and it gives you a chance to study the game in depth. Not many pitchers have a chance at becoming a manager, a job I wouldn't mind, but more than any other starting players, pitchers are able to study the game and learn what managers have to know.

THE IMPORTANCE OF PITCHING

Many managers believe that pitching is 90 percent of the game, but when you talk about its importance—whether you agree with the 90 percent figure or 75 percent or whatever—you also have to take into consideration how good your defense is.

The excellent record of our Oriole pitchers is attributable, to a great degree, to our outstanding defense. Our fielders—Brooks Robinson and the others—make our pitching better. That's why a Pat Dobson, whose record was 14–15 with San Diego, could come to the Orioles and chalk up a 20–9 record. He was probably the same pitcher in both places, but with us he had more confidence. Our defense picked him up and made him a better pitcher. Our four Golden Glovers definitely make it a lot easier to pitch.

By the same token, you can't really compare a pitcher with, say, the Texas Rangers, an inexperienced team defensively, with a pitcher on our staff.

The relative importance of pitching to a ball club also depends on the team's hitting. For instance, pitching is less important on an excellent offensive ball club like the Cincinnati Reds than on a weak-hitting team. The Pittsburgh Pirates have thrived for a number of years on great hitting and poor pitching. The opposite condition existed with the Los Angeles Dodgers, whose success for years revolved around the pitching of Don Drysdale and Sandy Koufax. The Mets got all the way to the World Series in 1973 on the pitching arms of Seaver, Koosman, McGraw, and Matlack. Everybody knocks Vida Blue for not winning the "big" ball games, but you can't very well fault a guy for his pitching when he loses 2–0. It's just a matter of his club not getting runs.

It's rare that a team is good both on offense and defense, but there have been such instances. The Orioles of 1969, 1970, and 1971 had outstanding pitchers and good hitters, and the Oakland A's now have an outstanding defense, great power, and a tremendous pitching staff. Imagine how good the Pirates would be if they had the pitching to go with their hitting!

GOOD PITCHING VS. GOOD HITTING

In general, I believe in the axiom that good pitching stops good hitting (except in the case of a *super*-hitting ball club). In the 1970 World Series against the Reds, we probably had one of the best pitching staffs ever assembled, yet they still managed to score three and four runs a game. It was only because they had such a poor pitching staff that we were able to outscore them.

On the other hand, one of the better-hitting teams we faced was Pittsburgh, in the 1971 World Series. There was some decent scoring in a few of the games, but the pitching on both sides essentially handcuffed the hitting. We lost the Series in the seventh game, 2–1. Mike Cuellar pitched a great game for us, but that particular year the late Roberto Clemente had a great Series and provided the winning edge for the Pirates.

ABILITY—NATURAL AND OTHERWISE

THE NATURAL ARM

I mentioned before the importance of having a good arm if you hope to be a successful pitcher. There are players born with great arms who don't necessarily become pitchers. A player like Reggie Smith can throw the ball 350 feet on the line. Then again, there are some major-leaguers who, believe it or not, have to be *taught* to throw properly. Don Baylor, an outfielder with the Orioles, doesn't have a naturally fluid motion, so he had to be taught.

Your muscular build has a lot to do with your natural

pitching ability. There are exceptions, but most pitchers are rather lanky and have long arms. Whatever your build, you need a tremendous amount of leverage and excellent coordination to pitch.

You can probably identify the most notable examples of the natural pitcher, the players born with fantastic arms and blessed with good wrist motion and eye-arm coordination besides.

Nolan Ryan has fluid motion and a great arm. So do Gibson, Seaver, and Carlton, Jim Hunter, Dave McNally, Vida Blue, and Bert Blyleven. Mike Cuellar, meanwhile, is a perfect example of a pitcher with a great arm who learned to pitch differently. Today all his stuff is "manufactured," you might say. He doesn't get by with his natural stuff any more and yet he's still a very successful pitcher. Mike's story is an excellent illustration of a point you should realize about pitching: a pitcher always looks to improve himself, no matter how far he's come. Always.

Don't other players always look to improve themselves? you might ask. Certainly. But there's a difference in this regard between a pitcher and a hitter. A hitter who finished a season with ten home runs and a .250 batting average will want to hit fifteen home runs next season, but may not worry about improving his average by perhaps becoming a spray hitter and hitting to all fields.

By contrast, a pitcher—especially one on a ball club that stresses pitching—will be told by his pitching coach after his first year: "We're going to add a pitch. We're going to work on a slider. You didn't throw it last year, so it will give the hitters something new to look at. Even if you don't get it over, you'll be able to throw it in some situations when you're ahead of the hitter, and then he'll have to look for it at other times. So it will make your other pitches look better."

The pitcher will do just that, and his whole pitching ability will improve.

Mike Cuellar was doing this sort of thing as far back as ten years ago. Even though he had a good fast ball and a pretty good curve, he was working on his screwball. Then he came up with a slider, and now he even throws a change-up—actually a palm ball—as well, so now when he pitches, a hitter looks at five different pitches.

WHEN YOU DON'T HAVE GREAT NATURAL ABILITY

So much for the fellows with excellent natural ability. If you've got it, be grateful, and do your best to capitalize on it and improve it.

If you don't have outstanding natural ability, there's no cause for despair. Working within the limits of your natural ability, you can still develop yourself into a pretty fair pitcher.

Fritz Peterson of the Indians doesn't have outstanding natural ability, but he came up with a knuckle curve, as well as a change-up and slider—and he hardly ever walks anybody. He realizes that his talent is going to allow him to do only a certain number of things, so he knows he can't afford to put men on base unnecessarily. Accordingly, he's worked on his control and, except for 1973, has had many good years.

THROW WHAT YOU THROW BEST...

Working within your ability ties in with another principle to keep in mind: as a pitcher, throw what you throw best.

I don't mean that you should limit yourself exclusively to fast balls if you're a fast-ball pitcher—you can't be so predictable that the hitters will always know what's coming. But I do mean that generally you should rely on your special pitching ability, especially in tight spots. If you can't overpower a batter with a fast ball, don't try to. Throw what you throw best, to the spots where you're most effective.

For instance, I get most of my outs on high fast balls, so I don't often try to throw the ball low and away, as much as I'd like to be able to. Obviously, if I find I'm getting the ball up so much that I'm walking batters, I have to change. But if I can get ahead of the hitters and then pitch up, I think I'm most effective that way.

Of course, there are always exceptions, an excellent example of which took place during our 1973 playoffs against Oakland. In the fourth game I lasted a big two and a third innings, probably because I was a little tired from pitching the first game. Then I came back the next day in the fifth game and pitched five shutout innings. I really didn't have good stuff—in fact, it was probably no better than the day before, when I'd given up about half a dozen consecutive line drives—but this game I was making excellent pitches with my breaking pitch, of all things. I was getting the ball in the corner where I wanted it.

Another good example of an exception was the sixth World Series game against the Pirates in 1971. I found that, early in the game, every time I threw a fast ball it was hit pretty hard, and I felt I had to go to something else. It was funny; I was getting my curve ball over, and this allowed me to throw my fast ball and work on spots.

I got back in the groove and started making good pitches, and we won the game. My manager, Earl Weaver, said afterward that I'd had less stuff that game than in my previous Series start, and yet I'd pitched a better game.

Earl is always telling me to throw more breaking balls, but despite those notable exceptions—that sixth Series game and the fourth 1973 playoff game that I mentioned—I realize the percentage of breaking balls that I throw for strikes isn't anywhere nearly as good as the percentage of fast balls I throw for strikes. Besides, most of the time I can throw my fast ball where I want, to spots, while I'm happy just to throw my curve ball for a strike anywhere.

So, in general, I have to disagree with Earl (respectfully, of course) because I know the breaking ball is not the best pitch for me to throw; it's not my percentage pitch. Now, if I didn't have the raw natural ability that I do, I'd probably have a different outlook. And most probably, later on in my career, when I lose some of my natural ability, I will have to make some changes.

. . . AND DO YOUR OWN THING

People sometimes ask me whether I tried to copy particular major-league pitchers before I got to the big leagues. That goes back to what we were just discussing—the importance of doing your own thing.

I couldn't emulate Don Drysdale because I didn't throw the way he did, and, much as I would have liked to pitch like Juan Marichal, I soon discovered I simply wasn't a Juan Marichal.

Throughout my career, I *have* tried to *learn* from

other pitchers, including those who can do things that I can't—for instance, Bert Blyleven, who has a great curve ball and really follows through when he delivers, and Tom Seaver, who really drives and is very low to the ground. You do try to keep improving yourself by trying to do things differently. But if you're going good, don't try to change yourself.

I admire any pitcher who is a good all-around athlete. Of course, I also respect someone like Nolan Ryan, who, while not a good hitter, probably has the best pitching ability of anybody in baseball. Nobody throws harder than Nolan, and he has an excellent breaking ball as well; about the only thing he hasn't accomplished yet is excellent control. I admired Sandy Koufax because of his tremendous pitching talent when he was not a very good hitter or fielder, whereas his teammate, Don Drysdale, could do almost everything well. Tom Seaver doesn't have the *best* all-around ability, but he certainly knows how to pitch. Not only does he throw hard, he has a great breaking ball, and great control. Mel Stottlemyre is another pitcher I admire.

Bob Gibson, who's had a fantastic career, can do everything. He can hit, he can field, he can run. I guess if there's anyone I try to pattern myself after, it's Bob, because I always was proud of the fact that I could hit better than most pitchers, and I could field. Even though I haven't won the Golden Glove, I honestly think I can field as well as any pitcher in baseball today, and the Orioles use me as a pinch runner.

I'm not mentioning this to brag, but simply to point out that if you must try to model yourself after a big-league pitcher, set your sights on someone who is a complete player and someone whose style of play is like your own.

Equipment and Other Aids

EQUIPMENT

YOUR GLOVE

Your glove is a vital part of your equipment for two reasons—your pitching and your fielding.

For pitching, you want your glove to be big enough so you can put your entire hand into it when you're gripping the ball for a pitch. This helps you disguise your intention, which is important because you don't want the batter to be able to guess what pitch you're intending to throw. For the same reason, the web of your glove should be solid, so the hitter can't catch a glimpse of the ball through it.

While you want your glove to be big, you don't want it to be so cumbersome that you feel you can't catch the ball comfortably, or that when the ball lands in the glove you won't be able to find the "handle" on it right away.

I use a Spalding model. Whatever brand you select, you'll find that an outfielder's glove is the biggest one

Your glove should be big enough so that you can put your entire hand into it when you're gripping the ball for a pitch. This helps you keep the batter from guessing what pitch you intend to throw.

made and big enough for a pitcher's purposes. In selecting a glove, don't be swayed by the player's autograph on it. You're not going to pitch like him just by using the glove he's endorsed.

When I'm pitching, I keep my middle finger outside the glove, something that a lot of pitchers find comfortable. But you decide what's comfortable for you.

Breaking In Your Glove. I think the biggest thrill I ever had as a child was getting a new glove and breaking it in. I'd put a baseball in it and tie it up, and put it under the breakfront or somewhere similar. Often, I'd even put it underneath my mattress and sleep on it. Major-leaguers break in their gloves in different ways.

Most gloves come with a lot of padding in the heel. Because I like to have a nice round pocket, I'll usually take a little of this padding out, just by undoing the rawhide at the bottom of the glove, then laying the glove on the ground and pounding the pocket with a bat. Besides helping to round out the pocket, the pounding serves an additional purpose: it keeps the glove from folding on me, as it would if it were flat.

Care of Your Glove. During the average season, I'll probably use two gloves and start breaking in a third. I put saddle soap or something like it on the gloves to clean them and make them soft. I don't oil them very often.

Besides affecting a glove's appearance, dirt will also affect the breathing capacity of the leather. So it's wise to bring your glove in with you from the field after each half inning. That way the sun won't crack the leather, the dirt it picks up will be minimal, and the glove won't be stepped on.

Storing Your Glove. When I put my gloves away for the winter, I put a baseball in each and wrap them up. I don't put covers on them because it's fairly dry where we spend our winters. When you put your glove away for the winter, try to store it in a fairly dry place, if possible. Putting it into a plastic bag isn't a bad idea, because that will provide a little moisture and not allow the leather to dry out too much.

What really ruins a glove is the humidity. It gets so

soggy and wet, especially in the summer, that often after I've pitched with one glove I have to use another one to shag flies.

BALLS

Be sure to play and practice with a regulation ball, so that you're always working with balls that are the same in size, compactness, and content. In spring training before the 1974 season, some clubs found that even weak hitters were banging the covers off the balls, which were now being made of cowhide instead of horsehide. This was a defect in manufacturing that was soon corrected.

A scuffed or used ball is preferable because (1) you can grasp it better to make it do more things (curve or break), and (2) the scuff marks provide some air resistance, to make the ball move more.

I prefer one of the infielders doing the rubbing up because it takes a lot of strength to rub up fifty different balls a game, and the pitcher should save his strength for pitching. Fortunately, the balls in the major leagues are already rubbed up.

THE RESIN BAG

One of the pitching aids some pitchers like to use is a resin bag. It's great for your breaking ball because it gives your fingers a sticky feeling and helps your feel of the ball. I use it in the heart of the summer when I perspire a lot, because it absorbs the perspiration and doesn't make my hand as slick as it would be otherwise. In cold weather, though, I don't like to use it at all because my hand doesn't sweat as much, and the resin just doesn't mix with the amount of perspiration my hand has then.

SOCKS AND SHOES

Because, as we'll see, the feet are so important to pitching, you want to take care of the socks and shoes that go on them.

Obviously, your shoes must fit correctly, which is true of any footwear you use for athletics. In pitching, you do as much work with your feet and legs as you do with your arms. There's so much pressure on your feet because of all the pushing off you do, your shoes must be comfortable.

Despite the punishment that some parts of my feet absorb in a game, I don't wear extra socks. Occasionally, though, I will bandage those parts of my feet that get most of the pressure—such as the toes of the front foot, which will slide a little when the front cleat lands. Sometimes I'll also bandage the ball of my right foot, which drags across the dirt when I pitch. On certain mounds, where the dirt is a little high in front of the rubber, it's possible to get bruised. Bandaging helps to prevent this.

A toe plate built into pitcher's shoes does relieve some of the pressure. Make sure to wear the toe plate on your right foot.

Many major-leaguers have taken to wearing rubber-type cleats or soccer-type shoes, especially because of the artificial turf. I wear a metal-type cleat all the time a game is in progress, although I do my between-game running in my plastic-type, soccer-foot shoe because it's light and comfortable.

Care of Your Shoes. I keep my shoes polished and I generally put shoe trees in them so they won't curl up when they're wet.

YOUR SWEATSHIRT

It's imperative that you wear a sweatshirt, one that's substantial enough to keep your body warm and loose enough to give you freedom of motion. You shouldn't wear anything that's going to restrict your motion.

I prefer a heavy one, duo-ply cotton, so that my body does not perspire and then cool off. I hurt my back in Aberdeen, South Dakota, by wearing a light shirt, perspiring, cooling off, and then trying to pitch.

Length of sleeve varies. I like to wear a sweatshirt that's cut either just above the sleeve of the uniform, or a really long one down to my wrist. For some reason, a partway sleeve bothers me. In the big leagues, at least, the rules dictate that both sleeves of your sweatshirt have to be the same length.

By the way, all your clothing, from top to bottom, should be clean. If not, you risk infection and the possibility of offending your teammates.

FIELD AND PLAYING CONDITIONS

Something else a pitcher has to contend with is the field he's playing on, as well as the peculiar characteristics of each ball park.

THE MOUND

The condition of the mound is bound to affect your performance. It's most difficult to pitch in a light drizzle or when it has just stopped raining, mainly because the footing is bad. To deliver properly, you should be able to push off and land without your foot sliding all over. On a wet mound you can't push off as much. And, normally, if you have dirt in your cleats, you can kick the rubber and the dirt will fall out, but mud doesn't. It adheres to the bottom of your shoes, and when your front foot lands, it slides a little and hurts not only your control but also your mental outlook. Often, too, rain affects your grip on the ball. You can't dry your hand off if your uniform is soaked.

What can you do about a slippery mound? Adjust as best you can. Move a little more gingerly than normal.

FIELD DIMENSIONS

How big a ball park is, how far it is to the fences, and so on are things that probably shouldn't affect the way you pitch—but they do. The biggest effect the dimensions of a field have is on your mental outlook.

You feel you can afford to make fewer mistakes in Detroit and Boston, where the outfield fences are close to home plate, than, say, Baltimore or Yankee Stadium, so you try to keep all your pitches away from hitters in those smaller parks. Yet I've learned from experience that in Boston most of the hitters look for the pitch away because they're so accustomed to having pitchers throw to them that way. Thus they become susceptible to pitches inside.

In Yankee Stadium the Yankees put up primarily a left-hand hitting attack against right-hand pitching to take advantage of the short right-field porch. Those hitters would be out over the plate looking for a ball to pull, so you'd want to pitch to them differently, throw them breaking balls. In Boston, too, I try to throw low-and-away breaking balls to the right-handers, because any ball in the middle of the plate (but not *way* in) is a ball they can pull off the fence.

The greatest psychological effect that a field's dimensions can have on you is to make you try to do things that you don't ordinarily do. You may have just come off a successful game, where you pitched a five- or six-hitter, and because you pitched in a park that was relatively spacious, you didn't worry that much about a hitter pulling the ball. (Of course, you don't want him to pull it down the line, which is the easiest place to hit a home run, but you don't consciously make every pitch on the corner.) Yet when you go to Boston, you say to yourself, "I have to make every pitch perfect." The result is what is probably a pitcher's number-one hazard: you get behind the hitters and then you have to come across with a pitch they can cream.

When we clinched the pennant in 1971, Earl Weaver was asked which club he preferred to face in the World Series. He replied, "I'm mercenary. I root for the biggest park." So do his pitchers.

ARTIFICIAL TURF

Artificial turf affects a pitcher's performance—for good and bad.

It allows you to throw more double-play pitches, but you don't have double plays unless men are getting on base. One reason they are is that artificial turf is definitely advantageous to a hitter. Unless he hits a fly ball, his chances of getting a base hit on turf are much greater than on a grass field. Because the ball has overspin, it will skip through the artificial infield or go through the gap in the outfield more quickly. The result is not only more base hits, but more doubles and triples.

On turf, the ball gets hit back to the pitcher more quickly, which makes him more likely to be hit by the batted ball or less likely to field it. Bob Gibson still wins the Golden Glove for fielding, but he's told me he doesn't field as many of the balls as he used to. This is because, thanks to artificial turf, they're by him, either cut off by the infielders, or through for singles. And, since more men on base means more runs, it's certainly an advantageous surface for the hitters.

Psychologically, too, the batters know that if they hit the ball hard on the ground, they're going to have more chances to get more hits. But then again, if they hit it right at somebody, the ball will be hit so sharply it's likely to turn into a double play.

A lot of sinker-ball pitchers were adversely affected by the advent of artificial turf, because they knew that when a sinker was hit, the ball would be drilled hard through the infield. This is why some sinker-ballers have gone from the National League to the American League, where artificial turf is not as predominant.

When the White Sox installed their infield of artificial turf, we went in there and averaged about twelve runs a game. That turf really hurt their club, because they had Tommy John, Joe Horlen, and Gary Peters, all basically low-ball pitchers, who were suddenly being hurt by a fast infield. On a grass field, on the other hand, a ball hit on the ground often goes for a double play or at least one out.

On grass fields, too, the height of the grass has an effect. Milwaukee had one of the highest infields and one of the

25

lowest earned run averages. I think they were second or third to us in ERA one year. Then they cut the grass down and their earned run average shot up.

Artificial turf has an effect on legs as well. We don't run nearly as much in Kansas City as we do elsewhere. The turf has a different feel and it affects players' knees and shins. You don't want to do something in Kansas City, like suffer a shin split, that will hurt you when you go to Oakland. So we run less. Luckily, mounds aren't artificial, so a pitcher on the mound is spared the strain on the legs that other players suffer.

Also, the heat factor is something you can't escape. One of the few games I've pitched on artificial turf was the 1970 All-Star Game that I started in Cincinnati. I pitched three innings and I've never been so tired in my life. It was the middle of the season, and I was in shape; I was well rested after having three days off. But at the end of three innings, the humidity and the added heat given off by the turf were so great that when I laid down a perfect bunt and ran as hard as I could to first base, I felt almost as if I were standing still. The day before, I had been shagging flies in 85-degree weather there—and the turf was so hot I couldn't stand in one place.

WIND

Other physical playing conditions affect you, too. For instance, I adjust my pitching to wind conditions. It's just a psychological thing to start with, but it has eventually a physical effect. If you know the wind is blowing in, you realize you just have to throw strikes and not walk anybody. But if the wind is blowing out, you might try to pitch a little finer, be sure you make better pitches, maybe try to keep the ball down a little better. It's like the difference between pitching on artificial or natural turf. On the slow grass, you might really concentrate on keeping the ball down. Similarly, when the wind is blowing out to right field and you're facing a left-handed hitter, you'll want to pitch the ball away so that he hits to left field. You know that if he hits the ball well, the wind is going to keep the ball in the park.

SUNLIGHT AND SHADOWS

Sunlight and shadows don't have too much of an effect on your pitching, although in some parks, such as Yankee Stadium, it's really tough to pick up the ball visually. In Baltimore, on the other hand, I've found it very easy to pitch in the afternoon because there are white row houses out beyond center field. An overhand pitcher, especially a right-hander, seems to the batter to be throwing right out of those houses. As a result, I've been very successful, and haven't had to change anything in my windup or delivery. Some of our own hitters have been critical about the fact that nothing has been done to block out the all-white background those houses present. But it doesn't bother me or the other pitchers at all.

HUMAN AID AND COMFORT

There are several key people on any ball club who are most intimately involved with a pitcher's performance. Let's take a couple of minutes to discuss them.

THE MANAGER

A manager's importance to a pitcher shows up in such things as the decisions he makes in regard to how the pitcher is pitching—such as when to take him out of a game, and whether to hold him back to face a team against which his style would be more effective. (We don't do that much on the Orioles because we have a pretty well-balanced staff, which can get both right- and left-handed hitters out.)

An important aspect of a manager's effectiveness is what he says when he comes out to the mound. He has to know whether that particular pitcher needs to be motivated, whether he needs a pat on the back or some stronger type of encouragement. Chances are your manager (or coach) knows what you react to best, and treats you accordingly when you run into difficulty on the mound.

Generally, a manager can best help a pitcher by realizing what his strengths and weaknesses are, and by trying to help him channel those strengths most effectively, rather than telling him to try something of which he really isn't capable.

To tell the truth, many managers tend to underestimate the difficulty of pitching. They find it easier to believe that a guy has a fantastic arm and all he has to do is wind up and throw the ball over the plate. But obviously, pitching is a lot more complex and difficult—so many different factors can cause you to throw the ball high or low, inside or outside. Pitchers realize how hard it is to be a hitter because most get a chance in the batter's box. But managers, unless they were once pitchers themselves, don't get to pitch, and thus don't understand the intricacies of pitching.

Our manager, Earl Weaver, who was a good defensive second baseman, has a very good "book" on the hitters we face—he knows their strengths and weaknesses—so he's always helped me out in that respect. Sitting on the sidelines, he can see what kind of pitches the batters hit. Often a batter will hit one of your pitches that you thought was low but actually wasn't. You thought it was thigh-high, when actually it was belt-high. Managers can help you by pointing this out.

Too often, though, when managers conduct pitching meetings, where you talk about how to deal with particular hitters, their advice comes down to either "high and tight" or "low and away." It's a lot more complicated than that.

Once when Hank Bauer was our manager, we went over the Kansas City lineup, and when we got to Bill Bryan, a catcher who was a left-handed hitter with a fondness for low fast balls, Bauer's instructions were just to "spin it up there to him." In a crucial part of the game, with two strikes on the batter, our pitcher, Wally Bunker, did just that. He spun a belt-high curve up to Bryan, and Bryan clouted one of the longest home runs I've ever seen. When Bunker came into the dugout, Bauer asked, "How could you possibly do that?" and Wally answered, "You told me just to spin it up there."

Some managers—and catchers—call games as if they were batting, and on the basis of what type of pitch they wouldn't be able to hit. For example, if they couldn't hit a slider themselves, that's what they'd want you to throw.

But where a manager helps me most is in his ability to tell me what the other manager is thinking.

Let me give you an example. In 1973, in spring training, I was pitching against the Yankees. Bobby Murcer was up at bat, and Roy White was on first, and I kept throwing over to first because I guessed he'd be running. Because I thought Murcer would be looking for a fast ball, I was throwing him curves. But continually throwing over to first ruined my concentration, and I ended up getting behind Bobby. I threw him a fast ball and he hit a two-run homer to beat us, 2–1.

Weaver said to me, "You should have concentrated on the hitter because Ralph Houk (then the manager of the Yankees) usually tries to go for the big inning with Bobby Murcer up there in that kind of situation. When they're one run down, they want to go for two runs. They don't just want to tie the ball game up."

I'd never thought about it, but if I had, I would have realized the wisdom of Weaver's comment. If I'd known as much about Houk's strategy as Weaver did, I wouldn't have worried about the Yankees sending White down. I'd have realized they were going for two runs.

THE PITCHING COACH

To a pitcher in the major leagues, the pitching coach is even more important than the manager.

The pitching coach helps you not only during the ball game but with inside tips in between starts. For example, he may suggest that you develop a new pitch for your repertoire, and he'll tell you how to throw that pitch. He'll also correct you in what you're doing wrong and point up what you're doing right. And he'll demonstrate better ways of pitching. On our ball club, the pitching coach, George Bamberger, is a vital factor in our conditioning program because he directs us and makes sure we do it properly.

During a game, he'll point out anything we're doing that has a bad effect on our pitching. If, for instance, we're throwing the ball high, he'll be the one to point out that we've been overstriding. Or it may be a different problem—not striding enough or not following through, releasing the curve ball too soon or "You're rushing your delivery."

In the big leagues, where pitching coaches are very competent, it's very seldom that you get *wrong* advice. The only problem is that sometimes you get too *much* advice. One person tells you to do it one way, someone else tells you to do it differently, and it's tough enough to do what comes naturally.

It's good to have a pitching coach to confide in, and to let him be the one to tell you what to do. At your age, it's probably best to take the advice of the man managing or coaching your team. Now, in all honesty, while some coaches are very nice, and are interested in helping young people with sports, they are not especially knowledgeable in baseball. As you mature and experiment, your experiences will tell you how much of the advice you receive is valid.

YOUR TEAMMATES

If you're lucky, there will be veterans on your team who will help you with good advice. I was only nineteen when

I joined the Orioles.* I came to a club that had a lot of veterans, including Stu Miller and my first roommate in baseball, Robin Roberts. Robin and I were similar pitchers—fast ballers without that much of a breaking ball. His axiom was never to walk anybody, and he was pretty successful in that direction, although he did throw something like thirty-nine home run balls a year. He was a good roommate.

All in all, it was a great ball club for learning how to pitch. Besides Stu and Robin, we had Harvey Haddix, a great tutor. He was thirty-eight, twice my age, and had broken into organized baseball when I was about minus two or three years old. We also had Dick Hall, who'd been around and was very intelligent, and Harry Brecheen, a fine pitching coach. My nickname was "Brash" because I wasn't afraid to say what I felt—or to ask questions. It won't hurt you or your pitching career to ask questions of people who can give you helpful answers.

RELIEF PITCHERS

They're called "firemen," and while you're not always glad to see them coming, in a real baseball emergency a relief pitcher is the starting pitcher's best friend.

What a Reliever Needs. To be a successful relief pitcher, a hurler needs nerves of steel and a rubber arm. He also has to have one or more of the following: (1) a very good double-play pitch, such as a hard slider or good sinker; (2) the ability to strike out a lot of hitters; (3) excellent

* At age twenty years, eleven months, Jim became the youngest pitcher to win a complete World Series shutout game, in 1966.

control. If he has two or all three of these qualities, so much the better.

He also needs steady nerves, because he's almost always coming into a game in a pressure situation, so to do his job he's going to have to be able to withstand pressure.

Relievers don't have the luxuries that starters enjoy. A starting pitcher can get himself into a little bit of trouble, then recover and manage to work out of it. He may realize he doesn't have his curve ball and start relying on his fast ball, then later on in the game work his way back to the curve. A relief pitcher has to come in and do the job —put out the fire—right then.

Since most relievers are called upon to pitch two or three days in a row, a relief pitcher can't have an arm that tightens up on him. Although he didn't pitch many innings, Darold Knowles of the A's relieved in each of the seven games of the 1973 World Series. Of course, there have been outstanding exceptions. One is Dick Hall, who did an outstanding job for the Orioles despite the fact that he couldn't pitch more than one day without rest. He would pitch perhaps only every fourth day, but since he had pinpoint control and could strike men out, he did great work.

Should You *Be a Reliever?*   Whether you should deliberately set out to become a relief pitcher depends a lot on your physical makeup, as well as what sort of delivery you have and whether or not you have the qualities just discussed.

One question you might ask yourself is how long you can throw hard. Pete Richert started for a number of years, but then late in a game he'd kind of run out of gas, consequently giving up between thirty-six and forty home runs a year. Then he went into relieving, and was an excellent relief pitcher because he could throw hard enough and was overpowering enough for two or three innings to do the job.

Sidearm pitchers tend to make excellent relievers. They're essentially specialized and, except for an outstanding pitcher like Ewell Blackwell, don't have enough different pitches to be starters. A sidearm pitcher usually throws just a slider and a fast ball.

Darold Knowles is an example of a left-handed sidearmer who's brought in against lefties. He's got a pretty good sinker, but a right-handed hitter can pick up the ball pretty well on him. Dick Raddetz, who threw from somewhere between sidearm and three-quarters, and Horatio Peña, who is about as close as you can come to a submarine (almost underhand) pitcher, are righties who are brought into ball games mainly against right-handed batters for the same reason.

The biggest factor in the effectiveness of a Peña or of a Ted Abernathy, a submarine-ball pitcher who played for the Cubs for many years, is that batters don't get to see pitchers like them very often. The result is that a hitter will come back to the bench after an at-bat and report, "He showed me something different." Because the ball behaves differently from what the hitter expects, the man throwing it is generally successful.

No Insult to Be a Reliever.   Relief pitching is certainly an honorable occupation. The Cy Young award is given annually to the best pitcher in each league. In 1974, the National League's Cy Young award went, for the first time, to a *relief* pitcher—Mike Marshall of the Los Angeles Dodgers, who appeared in more than a hundred games! I don't think it would be any blow to my ego to be asked to be a reliever. Early in my career I was used as one. During the 1965 season I probably relieved twenty-five times, and even as recently as 1973 I was credited with a save. When Vida Blue came back to action after a long layoff, he was moved to the bullpen. You get used to it. Of course, you have to change your ways. For instance, you have to warm up and get loose more quickly, which is generally not a problem when you're young. Your arm has greater elasticity then, but later on in your career it tightens up a bit, so warming up requires more time. For this reason, at age thirty-seven, Mike Cuellar, for instance, would not be the ideal relief pitcher.

Some of my most memorable experiences came as a reliever. I remember a Labor Day double-header in my first year. The Yankees were leading us, 2–0, and I was brought in with the bases loaded. I struck out Mickey Mantle, Roger Maris, and Elston Howard to end the inning. That was quite a thrill. I ended up striking out eight men in five innings of relief. Curt Blefary hit a two-run homer to tie up the game, and Andy Etchebarren, who had just come up to us from the minors, put us ahead with a three-run, inside-the-park homer. Then Bill Stafford, pitching out of the shadows at Yankee Stadium, knocked me down on the next pitch.

The Complete Game.   Pitching a complete game, without having to be relieved, is a satisfying accomplishment. Pitchers who have many complete games to their credit either have outstanding ability or are sufficiently crafty and talented to be able to pitch well when they lose some of their stuff. Not all pitchers can do this. Nolan Ryan, for instance, is an overpowering pitcher, but he runs into trouble when he loses his fast ball. Vida Blue, too. Yet Jim Hunter and Dave McNally, among others, have the control and savvy to pitch well even when they don't have outstanding stuff, and they can also pitch well late in the ball game. I think a big turning point in my own career was when I learned to pitch fairly well when my stuff wasn't as good as it normally is.

If you're lucky enough to pitch for a high-scoring ball club, you're going to stay in games longer than you would if your team isn't scoring well. But whether or not you're with a high-scoring team, it's inevitable that in some games you're going to have to be yanked.

Knowing When to Come Out of a Game.   It's hard to say for sure who's the best judge of when a pitcher should be taken out of a game. A good manager is usually a good judge, and so is the catcher who can detect very clearly the difference between your first-inning pitching and, say, your seventh-inning performance.

You yourself should know when you've had it, and face up to it—that is, if you're honest with yourself and realistic about how the game and your pitching are going. I try to be a realist—I know when my stuff is not as good as it normally is—but I have to admit there have been times when I've convinced a manager to let me stay in and then regretted it.

Once when Hank Bauer was our manager, I had a 4–2 lead over Washington when Paul Casanova hit the ball back to me. I tried to barehand the ball but couldn't, and that put two men on, including the tying run. Bauer came out to the mound and asked, "How do you feel?" I threw a couple of trial pitches and my hand still stung, but I told the skipper I was all right. The Senators (who are now the Texas Rangers) put up a pinch hitter named Don Lock, who was a really good fast-ball hitter but supposedly couldn't hit anything that was spinning. The first pitch I threw was a curve and he simply creamed it into the left-field bleachers for a three-run homer, to give them the lead, 5–4. So I was one run down because I just hadn't looked at the situation realistically. I should have told my manager to take me out of the game because my hand hurt.

As I've matured and my career has blossomed, I look at things differently. I know my limitations and I'm not afraid to be frank about telling my manager when I just don't have it. Earl Weaver, our current manager, is pretty decisive about things like removing a pitcher from a game. But there have been times—the fourth playoff game in 1973 was one—when I've wished he'd taken me out sooner than he did.

A pitcher has to know what he can do on a particular day and, even though you'd like to pitch as often and as long as you can, there are situations when you realize it might be better if someone were to relieve you. So it shouldn't bother you to realize someone's warming up in the bullpen. There's no use continuing in a game when you no longer can help the ball club.

Waiting for Relief. It isn't necessarily impolite not to wait for the reliever to reach the mound, but it's certainly bad form for you to leave before the manager tells you to.

37

When Mike Marshall was with the Expos, he was brought into the first game of a 1971 twi-night double-header with the Cardinals in the seventh inning. He gave up the tying run in that inning, but then threw four excellent innings. In the top of the twelfth, Marshall was tagged for a couple of runs before a double play got him out of trouble. He grabbed his jacket at the bench and headed down the foul line to the dressing room. In the bottom of the twelfth the Expos started to rally, and pitching coach Cal McLish asked for Marshall. But he had departed. "He just moved from relief pitcher to manager in one step," said Gene Mauch, the manager, who promised a stiff fine. "He wasn't thinking of the Expos." The pitcher brought in to replace Marshall eventually gave up the winning run to the Cardinals.

When I was in the minors, in one game the home-team manager in Rochester headed to the mound from the third-base dugout. He just reached the third-base line when the pitcher threw him the ball and headed right for the first-base dugout, and the tunnel leading to the clubhouse. That's kind of a funny scene—unless you're the offended manager or the pitcher who's going to be fined for that particular display of temperament.

THE CATCHER

If a relief pitcher is a starter's best friend, a catcher is his brother. The catcher and the pitcher are the two components of the battery, and how well the pitcher functions depends a lot on the catcher's abilities in many different areas.

An Emotional Spur. Often you'll be tired late in the

game and the catcher will egg you on to sustain your effort and energy, rather than let you relax a little bit, as you might want to. To do this most effectively, he has to know whether you respond best to a pat on the back, a word of encouragement, or to a little needling.

A catcher's leadership ability and personality are big factors in how much help he is to a pitcher. If he's a "gung-ho" guy who's always in the game, his spirit is likely to be contagious. The target he gives you and how well he moves behind the plate are very important, all part of the larger qualities of intelligence and knowledge of the game.

Your Target.   The visual target the catcher gives you is crucial. He can make you throw the ball where he wants you to. If he just sits behind the middle of the plate, you're going to throw the ball in the middle of the plate, and that is awfully dangerous. If he moves to the outer part of the plate and gives you a good target, where the glove is readily visible, you'll throw it there (providing you've been concentrating on him as you should). A good catcher will wait until the last instant to make his move, otherwise a base runner could pick up the spot where you're aiming the ball and transmit that information to the batter, or the batter himself could see the movement. So the catcher will give you a target over home plate and then move inside or outside, where he wants you to throw the ball.

His Throwing Arm.   If your catcher has a good throwing arm, it's obviously a big plus, especially if you have a big windup that gives base runners a good jump for a

39

possible steal. I'm in that category. In 1972 I had a 10–0 record with Johnny Oates (later traded to Atlanta) behind the plate. Because he threw so well, I never had to worry about holding runners on, and that took a lot of pressure off me.

He Knows You. If there's the good relationship there should be between you two, a catcher who has been working with you for some time gets to know your pitching as well as you do. Like Santa Claus, he knows when you've been bad or good. Andy Etchebarren, for instance, is very helpful to me. He knows when I'm not throwing with my normal delivery; if I've got arm trouble, he can see almost immediately that I'm favoring my arm. Catchers have to follow the ball so well, they can quickly determine whether a pitcher's motion is the same as usual, whether he's throwing from the same spot, and so on. Often a catcher will tell you something like "Get your arm up," or "You're dropping your arm on the curve ball."

In 1973 I had an 8–4 record and then pitched three bad games in a row. I was charged with two more losses, and my record was down to 8–6. Andy told me, "Your ball doesn't have any life. Are you throwing the ball with ease, or are you trying to overthrow?"

That was the time I had had the flu and lost about ten pounds, and the fact was that in trying to throw extra hard, I was negating any natural wrist action I had. I was just tensing up and overthrowing. Then Andy suggested, "Why don't you just move the ball out on your fingertips, and maybe you'll get more life on the ball." I took his advice and I struck out nine men in eight innings, had a good ball game otherwise, and went on to win ten games in a row—and the Cy Young Award.

He Knows the Hitters.   A catcher has to know the hitters as well as the pitcher does.

Ultimately you, the pitcher, have to make the final decision on what pitch to make. It's not best if you don't have confidence in what you're going to throw. Generally—at least on our team—the catcher calls the pitches and we have the "veto" power. In other words, I can shake off the sign when I don't think it's right. For example, if he calls for a slider low and away, and I think it will work, I throw it; if not, I'll shake it off until he signals for a fast ball. Through experience, a pitcher will feel what he can throw successfully in a given situation. There are games when I shake off signs quite often, but others when I shake off hardly any at all.

More than once, though, I've shaken off a sign and lived to regret it.

In 1973 I had a no-hitter going, when late in the game Earl Williams, our catcher that day, called for a fast ball. But I thought it was a good time to throw a slider, so I shook off the first sign and eventually threw the slider right where I wanted it. It was apparently right where the batter (George Hendrick) wanted it, too, because he hit the ball through my legs for a line-drive single right up the middle, for the only hit of the game.

When the Manager Calls the Pitches.   How often the manager calls the pitches will vary from team to team. It doesn't happen often on the Orioles, but it happens.

We had a series in Kansas City at a time when our

41

pitching staff was not doing so well. Over the course of three seasons—1969, 1970, and 1971—we had beaten K.C. something like twenty-three straight games, and we extended it in 1972, even though our pitching was very erratic. In the first game Mike Cuellar gave up four home runs, each blasted over 400 feet, but we won the game, 6–5. Then Dave McNally frittered away a 5–0 lead, and we had to come from behind to win, 9–7. The next night it was my turn.

A problem we'd been having was that every time we got two strikes on a batter we'd be indecisive, and the hitter would work the count until it was even and then get a base hit, and they'd get a couple of runs. In the third game I had a 5–0 lead in the bottom of the fifth inning, when Bob Oliver singled to right. I threw a hanging pitch to Amos Otis and he tripled off the top of the center-field fence. Then I went to two strikes on Lou Piniella and threw him a hanging curve that was literally over his head —and he hit it off the clock in left field.

Normally when the pitching coach comes out to the mound, you're going to stay in the game; when the manager comes out, you're usually removed. This time our manager, Earl Weaver, came running out and the first thing he said—not even talking to me, but to our catcher, Etchebarren—was "Andy, those are the worst pitches I've ever seen called." I protested. "Earl," I said, "it's not Andy's fault. He called for them, but I threw them"—two hanging pitches. "Palmer," the manager said, "I don't want to hear a word. From now on, every time we get two strikes on a hitter, you look over and I'll call the pitches."

Well, the next inning I got the first man out, but the

next man singled. Then I got two strikes on Ed Kirkpatrick, the left-hand-hitting catcher-outfielder. Remembering our skipper's orders, I looked over toward him, and he was whistling and signaling, "slider, slider." I thought that was an excellent pitch to call—except I didn't throw a slider. I hadn't yet thrown one in my career. But an order is an order, so I ended up throwing a slider. Andy and I couldn't decide where I should throw it, but finally we figured that low and away would be the best place. I threw it low and away, and Kirkpatrick hit a line drive smack off my right kneecap. The ball rolled between Brooks Robinson at third and Mark Belanger at shortstop for a single.

They brought the stretcher out for me and, as I was being carried off, Earl Weaver asked me, "Can you pitch any more?" I replied, "What does it look like?" to which he said, "That's good, because I'm bringing in Ed Watt." And as they took me off the field, I heard him say to Etchebarren, "You know, Andy, it wasn't your fault—it *was* Palmer's fault."

I guess if there's any moral to be drawn, it's that when things go wrong, blame the pitcher.

Signs. There are a lot of ways for a catcher to signal for a pitch. It doesn't matter what method you use, so long as the pitcher—and to a lesser degree the infielders—understand what he's signaling for.

He can give the sign just with his fingers—one being a fast ball, two a curve, and three a slider, with a wiggling finger to indicate a change-up. He can pump his fist once for a fast ball, twice for a curve, and so forth.

He can also give what are called "flaps." He pats or

slaps his right thigh for a fast ball, the left side of his leg for change-up, and the center of his leg for a curve ball. This system involves the risk of sometimes letting your opponents pick up the signal too readily.

A common signaling technique is called the "first-sign indicator." If the catcher signals with one finger, it means that the sign you're looking for will be the sign that follows immediately. If he uses two fingers, it will be the second sign that counts, and so on. Sometimes the catcher will touch his mask, which means it's the second sign, or his knee to indicate that it will be the third sign. These systems can also be used with fingers or hand pumps.

As to where the pitch should go, usually the catcher's target is enough. But there are times when, after he's given the signal for the pitch he wants, he'll also signal *where* he wants it—inside or outside, high or low.

When your opponents steal a sign, it's bound to give the hitter confidence. After all, knowing something is coming generally makes it easier to hit, even though there will always be *some* doubt in his mind. Sometimes, though, anticipating a particular pitch makes a hitter overanxious, so knowing what is due becomes a disadvantage rather than an advantage. Signs aren't stolen that often, however. The time you want to be especially careful about guarding your sign is at a crucial point in the game, when a base hit can hurt you. If there's any doubt about the sign, you can always consult with the catcher face to face, but that's normally not necessary if your signs are good.

Passed Balls. A passed ball—a pitch that gets by the

catcher and is charged as his error—is often the fault of the pitcher. Passed balls usually occur when an overpowering pitcher is on the mound. Unlike a slower-thrown pitch, which is relatively easy to handle, balls thrown with good stuff on them may move all over the place— one time, sail, the next time, tail. It will sink, it will go up—and so be harder to catch.

A passed ball can also be indicative of a catcher's deficiencies—or a missed sign by the pitcher.

Mound Conferences. When a catcher comes out to talk to a pitcher at the mound, the thing he'll usually ask is "How do you feel?" or "Are you all right?"

Sometimes it's a strategy matter. For instance, let's say you have first base open and the tying or winning run on second. "How do you want to pitch to this guy?" the catcher will ask you. And then he'll want to know whether you want your fielders to play any differently than they are because of what you're planning to throw. (More about this point in the section on strategy, page 153.) It's possible that the catcher has spotted something about the particular hitter. Possibly you've been pitching him away and now he's moved up in the box, and your catcher wants to make sure that you've noticed.

Or your catcher may just be trying to slow you down so that you get back into your normal rhythm. It so happens I prefer to pitch at a pretty fast pace, because it keeps my teammates on their toes and gives the hitters less time to think about the pitch. There are situations, however, when it might be good, even for a pitcher who likes to throw quickly, to slow his pace down.

HELP FROM ELSEWHERE

Pitchers have slumps the way hitters do, and there's usually a reason, even though it's often hard to uncover. Pitching coaches help. So do films—sometimes.

In Baltimore we take a lot of films. When things aren't going well with your pitching, you try to compare the films of your subpar performances with films of games that were good ones. When, however, I went through that post-flu stretch of three or four bad games in 1973, the films revealed no difference in what I was doing—although the hitters were certainly letting me know something was wrong. No, this time it was Etchebarren, my catcher, the human element, who helped me out of that slump. I'd lost about eight inches off my fastball after losing ten or twelve pounds because of a virus.

Delivery

A MANUFACTURER can have the best merchandise in the world, but if he can't deliver it when and where he wants it, it's just about worthless to him.

The same thing applies to pitching. You can have sensational stuff, but if you can't deliver it the right way, what good is it?

Let's get into how to deliver the pitching goods you have—probably the most important aspect of a pitcher's game.

WHAT IS THE DELIVERY?

Delivery is basically a combination of simple steps, which should flow together smoothly. Briefly:

You take the sign from the catcher with one foot (the right one in the case of a right-handed pitcher) on the rubber, the other foot nearby. You're facing the catcher.

Once you have the signal, you bring your other foot back past the rubber as you lift your hands over your head. Your weight shifts to that other foot (the left one for a right-handed pitcher). Ready to absorb all your weight, the foot on the rubber, which was pointing toward home plate, now pivots toward third base so that it's almost parallel with the rubber. At the same time, the back foot swings around in front of you and up in the air, "kicking" toward third base, as your left shoulder aims directly at home plate, and your hands come back in front of you at waist level.

Then your right arm goes back, ready to pitch; your left side opens up, so that your left shoulder and gloved hand swing toward the plate; your left foot is planted forward, pointing at the plate; and your right arm begins to deliver the ball.

The wrist hangs back behind the forearm, cocked to throw. Then, aiming for the catcher's glove, you snap off the pitch, pushing off the rubber with the instep of your right foot. You follow through so that your right hand finishes almost at your left knee, and your glove hand is ready to catch or deflect a ball hit right back at you.

You land on the balls of your feet, ready to go right or left to field the ball.

That, in brief, is the delivery. It's important enough to dissect and discuss it step by step.

DIFFERENT DELIVERIES

Basically, there are three different deliveries—the overhand, the three-quarters, and the sidearm.

48

Picture a clock as you face the pitcher. In the case of a right-handed pitcher, his arm is between eleven and twelve o'clock when he throws overhand, between ten and eleven when he throws three-quarter, and at about nine when he pitches sidearm.

Three-quarter and sidearm deliveries have certain advantages and disadvantages, depending on whether you're pitching against a right-handed or left-handed batter. For pitching to both types, without great advantage or great disadvantage, the overhand is best.

Let me give you some examples. A right-handed pitcher throwing sidearm to a right-handed batter has a definite advantage because the batter can't visually pick the ball up very well. Also, there's the fear factor: to the right-handed batter, it looks as if the pitcher is throwing the ball right at him.

There's a further advantage in the path of the ball, which comes from way out toward third base at a sharp angle across the plate. But one big disadvantage is that a left-handed batter can see the ball thrown that way very well. And whether you're throwing to a right-handed or left-handed batter, a breaking ball thrown sidearm will stay on the same plane throughout the pitch. It doesn't go down, it goes just across. So if the hitter recognizes that it's a curve ball, he doesn't have to worry about it dropping. He knows it's just going to swerve sideways.

It's almost impossible to throw a good curve ball from a sidearm delivery, and a good curve ball is something a right-handed pitcher absolutely needs to get good left-handed batters out. If you throw sidearm, you'll have to rely on a flat curve or a slider. (We'll get into details of particular pitches in a later chapter.)

Side and front view of an overhand delivery, which I prefer because I have the most success with it. I feel it's the best kind of delivery against either a right-handed or left-handed batter, without great advantage or disadvantage. If you picture a clock, the pitcher's hand is between eleven and twelve o'clock.

The three-quarter delivery shares some of the same pluses and minuses the sidearm does. For instance, fear also plays a part here because, to the hitter, the ball looks almost as if it's being thrown from behind him. But on the other side of the picture, it's hard to get your arm in the proper position to throw a curve ball from a three-quarter delivery. So most three-quarter pitchers (and side-armers) throw fast balls and sliders primarily. As a rule, they don't have excellent curve balls, although, as always, there are some exceptions. My ex-teammate, Dave McNally, a lefty, is one of the few three-quarter pitchers with an outstanding curve ball; I guess he was born with the ability. He throws a very hard one. Dave has some other things going for him, too: a fast ball that runs away really well from right-handed hitters and a very effective flat slider.

Throwing from the overhand position, you don't have any tremendous advantage against a right-handed hitter. The ball doesn't look as if it's being thrown from behind him, so he doesn't get frightened. But it is the best position from which to throw a fast ball, curve, and slider effectively. One thing I especially like about being a right-handed, over-the-top pitcher is that I don't have to worry as much about getting out left-handed hitters as a side-armer or three-quarter pitcher does. This is important, because many of the good hitters in the American League are left-handers.

Because they don't have the good slow-breaking ball to get left-handers out, some sidearm pitchers try to switch to a delivery that's slightly more on top when they pitch against left-handers. And some pitchers try to convert fulltime from their natural way of throwing. I don't recommend this.

Side and front view of a three-quarter delivery, in which the pitching arm is between ten and eleven o'clock. It's hard to throw a curve ball from a three-quarter delivery, but it has the advantage of making hitters from the same side feel as if the ball is almost being thrown from behind them.

When I was in high school, I used to throw sidearm and three-quarters as well as overhand, the way Juan Marichal did. But I wasn't a Juan Marichal and, as I got older, I found I couldn't throw from all those positions. I'd try to drop down to three-quarters on hitters and yet my position wouldn't be any different; all I'd do was take some of my natural stuff off the ball.

Now I occasionally drop down and throw sidearm, but normally I stay up on top, where I find my best ability is. So should you. Rather than throw three-quarters one time and sidearm another, you should try for what you might call "excellence of repetition." Do something as well as you can, as often as you can. Or to put it another way, stay with the natural delivery you throw with and try to develop that. I've seen some unfortunate results when "they" have tried to tamper with Mother Nature.

In the 1960 draft, we let Dean Chance go and kept Ernie Thorland. They had both played in the Appalachian Rookie League, and Chance had pitched a couple of no-hitters, but Thorland, who had struck out something like twenty-four out of twenty-seven men one game, was kept over Dean, so you can tell how much talent he had. When you strike out that many men, you must have pretty good stuff. But "they" weren't satisfied. They decided that if Thorland, who threw three-quarters, would bring his arm up on top and throw overhand, it would help him with his breaking ball. Well, they tried to change his delivery, he hurt his arm, and it was the last year he ever pitched successfully.

That illustrates what can happen when you try to change someone's natural delivery.

It's true, for instance, that if you throw sidearm, the

Side and front view of a sidearm delivery, in which the pitcher's arm is at
about nine o'clock. It's almost impossible to throw a good curve ball with
this kind of delivery, but even more than the three-quarters, it makes hitters from the same side of the plate fear the ball is being thrown from
behind them. But against a right-handed pitcher, a left-handed batter has
an easy time picking up the pitch.

left-handed hitters will be able to pick up the ball better. But that doesn't mean your coach should change you. If you have good natural ability and you can throw the ball hard and get it over the plate sidearm, you're going to have a pitching job. You might be a reliever, but there's certainly no disgrace in that. (Very few starting pitchers are sidearm pitchers because they normally have just two pitches, a slider and a fast ball.)

So stay with your normal delivery, because if you start moving your arm around to pitch from different positions, you'll start using different muscles and either strain muscles you normally don't use or put a different kind of stress on them. Eventually, you're going to hurt your arm.

Just develop the most natural way you can throw. If you throw sidearm and you can do the job that way, fine. There's no one set way or "right" way to do it.

Now let's get into the mechanics of delivering the ball.

STANCE

As you take your position on the mound, maybe wondering what to do and perhaps thinking you should have become an auto mechanic or a doctor instead of a pitcher, your first concern is how to stand on the rubber. This sets the pattern for the rest of your delivery.

Basically, there are three places you can put your back foot (the right one, if you're a right-handed pitcher) on the rubber—the center of the rubber, to the left of center, or to the right of center.

It doesn't much matter where you stand on the rubber, providing that your stance doesn't lead you into throwing

The rarest kind of delivery is the "submarine" or underhand variety, a side and front view of which are shown here. The pitcher's arm is at about eight o'clock.

across your body. That's one of the worst things a pitcher can do, because it doesn't give his hips a chance to open up, which is what provides much of a pitcher's power as he strides toward the hitter. A few sidearmers, such as Dean Chance and Steve Barber, can throw across the body successfully—mainly because the optical effect contributes to fear on the part of right-handed batters. For most pitchers, though, it should definitely be avoided.

I stand with my right foot a few inches right of center on the rubber. The front cleats of my right shoe rest on the dirt, and the back of those cleats are up against the front of the rubber so that the foot can't go back any farther.

Occasionally, when I have a problem getting the ball away, I may experiment moving one way or the other on the rubber, but essentially my right foot starts out a little to the right of center. Some right-handers will pitch from the left-hand corner of the rubber when they want to keep the ball away from a right-handed hitter. Because the rubber isn't that large—twenty inches across—that little bit of movement isn't likely to give anything away.

Where should *you* stand on the rubber?

In the position you feel most comfortable, and one that allows your left foot to land properly when you're going toward the plate. I always draw a line—I started doing this in high school—from the center of the rubber toward the plate. Then, when I complete my delivery, I can make sure—from my footprints—that my left foot is landing on the left side of that line. If it lands to the right of that line, it means I'm throwing across my body. (More about that a little later.)

Okay, I'm standing there with my right foot just a little

I stand with my right foot a few inches right of center on the rubber. The front cleats of my right shoe rest on the dirt and the backs of those cleats are up against the front of the rubber.

Improper positioning of feet in relation to the rubber results in faulty delivery.

to the right of center on the rubber. My left foot is off the rubber, almost even with the right foot but just a little bit to the front of it and the rubber. Most of my weight is on the right foot because that's the foot I'm going to have to turn and eventually drive off from.

At this stage in your delivery, the most important consideration is that you have good balance. And, of course, that you're in position to take the sign.

HOLDING THE BALL

As you lean forward to take the catcher's sign, there are many ways of holding your hands. You can hold the ball with your bare hand in your glove, which I think is the best way because it allows you to hide the ball pretty well. If you prefer, though, you can hold the ball in your pitching hand, behind your back or down at your side, or you can hold the ball just with your glove hand and then reach into the glove as you start your windup.

I put the glove in front of me about waist high, with my pitching hand holding on to the ball in the glove, and I start my windup from there. This prevents the hitter from seeing me change my grip on the ball.

Which way you do it isn't important in itself. But it's essential that you don't tip your pitches. Jesse Jefferson, a young pitcher on our ball club with fantastic ability, used to tip off batters to what pitch was coming in many different ways.

He'd hold the ball by his side in his pitching hand, and when he was going to throw his fast ball, he'd come up to his glove with his fingers on top. When he was going

As you lean forward to take the catcher's sign, you can (A) hold the ball with your hand in your glove, which I think is best because it allows you to hide the ball pretty well. Or (B) you can hold the ball just with your glove hand or (C) hold the ball in your pitching hand, behind your back or down at your side.

to throw his curve ball, he'd come up with white showing, which let hitters tell themselves, "When you see white, it's a breaking ball." Another way he tipped off his pitches was in his motion: he would rock back differently on his curve than he would on his fast ball; he'd become off balanced. I think he also held the ball differently for a curve and a fast ball, in a way that was visible to the batters.

Jesse came all the way through the minor leagues without being told that he was tipping his pitches about every possible way. In 1972 he pitched a game carried on national television, and Tony Kubek, the former ball player who is a sports commentator for NBC, was able to call every pitch he was going to throw. Apparently, so could our opponents, who hit him for about four home runs. Jesse went down to winter ball and concentrated on erasing those telltale signs. The biggest change he made was to start with his pitching hand on the ball in the glove as he went into his windup.

I throw all my pitches the same way, but many pitchers change the position of their fingers on the ball, depending on whether they're going to throw a fast ball, curve, slider, or whatever. If you're one of them, it's beneficial to start your motion with the ball in your glove and your pitching hand on the ball. Then, when you change your grip from *across* the seams to *with* the seams, it's not as obvious to the hitter as it would be if you were holding the ball just in your bare hand.

For the same reason, it's important to reach into the glove the same way each time. I didn't do this in high school, but I doubt whether the hitters were smart enough to pick it up. What I should have done, and what you

61

should do, is put your hand in so that it's almost entirely covered by the glove. If you do this, nobody can ever see whether your hand is turned to the side or straight or whatever.

Many pitchers hold the ball in the heel of the glove. But if you do it this way, the hitter can still see the white of the ball and whether your wrist is cocked to throw a curve ball or held straight for a fast ball. But if you hold the ball in the top of your glove, actually in the webbing, your wrist isn't visible. This is why I think a pitcher should have a pretty big glove, big enough to hold his hand in and hide the ball without being so cumbersome that he can't field a ball or defend himself if a line drive is hit back at him.

So have your pitching hand hold the ball in the webbing of your glove, the back of which is facing the batter and whose fingers are pointed skyward. Look in for your sign, and get ready to go into your windup.

THE WINDUP

Some fans, remembering how Don Larsen pitched a perfect game in the World Series, ask whether a windup is really necessary. I think it is because it's what gets your momentum going toward home plate. (And even though people speak of Larsen as having pitched without a windup, he really used one, except that he cut out some parts of it he didn't feel were necessary.)

I tried the Larsen approach in Clearwater, in the instructional league, in 1964 because I thought it would allow me to make my windup more compact. My coaches had thought I was leaning backward in my windup, and that not bringing the ball up over my head would help make me more compact and concentrate more on the catcher. But doing it, I just didn't feel I could throw as hard, because I didn't have that momentum going toward home plate.

A fault of many young pitchers when they go toward home plate is that they don't have any drive at all. Remember, just as a hitter awaiting a pitch cocks his hips backward and then opens them up as the bat comes through, the pitcher has to turn his hips to cock them, and then open them, along with his left shoulder and left arm, as he drives toward home plate. Your left shoulder and left hip opening up gives you your thrust and, boosted by the momentum of your legs, allows you to drive to home plate. It's your windup that gets you into proper position for your hips and shoulder to move properly. Don Larsen turned his hips and did almost everything else someone with a conventional windup does, except put his hands over his head. And that's not a "must."

TYPES OF WINDUPS

There are various ways for you to wind up. One way you can do it is the way Bob Gibson does, holding the ball behind your back, then taking it straight over your head and reaching up to meet with the glove at that point. In this style, you rock backward, put your hands over your head, and then go into your hip turn.

You can also hold the ball at your side or in front of you or even with your side—and then go over your head. Or you can start the way I do, from the glove, and then rock back while putting your hands, still together, over

63

your head. When they go into their windup with no one on base, most pitchers end up having their hands over their head. But some take their hands only as high as the face, rather than over the head.

Some pitchers give you a lot of motion, complete with rocking of the arms. It's just a matter of what feels best to you. So much of pitching is rhythm. Just as, with a golf swing, you have to start your club right, in pitching you have to get your body started the proper way. And to do this, you have to get into an established pattern, a set rhythm that's going to enable you to be on balance when you deliver the ball.

This rhythm varies from pitcher to pitcher, and occasionally with the same pitcher. I'd get to the point late in the season when I felt a little tired, and Davey Johnson, who was then our second baseman, would say, "Use your Bob Gibson windup." What he meant was that Gibson has such a fluid windup and his whole body is channeled toward home plate when he releases the ball.

Tom Seaver does it a little bit differently. He has a pretty compact windup, too, but he drives toward home plate with the thrust of his legs, whereas Gibson just about throws his whole body at the hitter. Nolan Ryan is a very powerful pitcher with a powerful windup and tremendous stride toward home plate. He has the same basic windup that I do, which is probably the most common type in the major leagues.

The style of your windup can have a big impact on a hitter. If you've got a herky-jerky motion, sometimes the hitter won't be able to follow the ball, while with a really fluid, smooth-flowing motion, the hitter may tend to relax and then suddenly find the ball is on top of him and he's not prepared. That's what hitters mean when they comment that a particular pitcher "doesn't throw that hard, but he's sneaky." The pitcher's motion is very relaxed (I think mine is), the hitter doesn't pick up the ball very well, and then suddenly the ball gets there before he really expects it to. Vida Blue has that effect.

YOUR BACKSWING

When you've taken the sign, you're ready to start your motion. The idea is to get your body into a position that will enable you to open up and deliver the ball with force and accuracy.

Remember that you started with your right foot on the rubber and your left foot off the rubber and just a trifle ahead. You were leaning in at the waist as you took the sign. Now two things happen almost at once: your left foot swings back past the rubber, just as your hands go over your head.

Some pitchers put their hands directly over the head; others put them a little to one side. I don't go way above —just barely—and I don't fully extend my arms.

Be sure that you're balanced when the left foot goes back and your weight transfers to it. Bring that left foot back as far as you can—as long as you can keep your balance—to get your body in a position from which you can start your move forward. I go back about twelve inches, which is a good distance if you can handle it. The more you go back, within the limits of your balance, the more momentum you'll have going forward. When I've been in a slump, I take a little more of a step backward and it helps me with more momentum going forward.

Once you've got that left foot back (we're still presuming you're a right-handed pitcher; lefties, just reverse the procedure), get set to transfer your weight back to your right foot, so you can start to make your turn and get in the proper position to deliver the ball.

At this point, about 95 percent of your weight is on your left foot. You're in a rocking-back position, and the only contact you have with the rubber is with the toe of your right foot. Your right heel is just about off the ground.

Nolan Ryan, incidentally, almost takes his right foot off the rubber at this stage of his delivery. There was some feeling that it should be called an illegal pitch when he does that.

In any event, when you rock back on your left foot, you should put almost all your weight on it. Then start turning your right foot to the right, along with your hips, getting in position to return all your pressure to your right foot and drive to home plate.

When you first started out, your right foot, the one on the rubber, was pointed pretty much straight at the plate. But now it pivots toward third base, so that it's almost parallel with the rubber and pressing against it. (Many pitchers like to throw with the right foot on an angle— the toes in front of the rubber and the heel on the rubber —but I find I lose my balance that way because my spikes don't get a firm grasp on the rubber. So I prefer having my foot parallel.)

YOUR KICK

As you pivot that right foot toward third base, your body pivots to your right along with it. Your weight returns completely to that right foot as you raise your left foot in

66

A high kick gives you more momentum, but with it you run the risk of being off-balance.

a kick. Your arms have come down to your waist.

This is the most important part of the windup. If you're falling back to the left, or you're too far to the right, you're not going to be in a balanced position to drive toward home plate.

You can kick high, low, or medium. Each has its advantage and disadvantage. It might be tempting, for instance, to follow Juan Marichal, who has a very high kick. But keep in mind that, while the high kick is likely to give you more momentum, the higher you kick, normally the more off-balance you get. Then, when it comes time to release the ball, you'll have to compensate by jerking your front shoulder down, with the result that your timing and effectiveness are off.

The left shoulder has to be level and pointing toward home plate when you release the ball. So if you rock way back, you're going to have a lot of difficulty getting that shoulder down in time to release the ball properly. With that shoulder way up, you'll feel as if you're throwing the ball almost straight up in the sky.

A low kick doesn't give you a balance problem, but it may not give you enough leverage to get the desired velocity on the ball.

A moderate kick, then, is probably the best. In the kick I use, which is considered fairly high, my knee goes about as high as my waist. It allows me to keep my balance and still give me the desired momentum to start my move toward home plate.

Not only don't you want your left shoulder too high in the air, you also don't want to turn it too far to the right. If you do, it will be out of proper position when you bring it around. The most important thing to try for is to have your left shoulder perpendicular to home plate. Then it will eventually go right *at* home plate. Our pitching coach always tells us the perfect guideline is to drive with your left shoulder directly at the catcher, who's normally sitting behind home plate.

You can experiment with your kick. If you want to get a little more leverage, rock back more. But again, remember the most important thing is to keep your left shoulder level and almost parallel to the ground. As you rock back, the right shoulder is going to be somewhat lower, but at release the left shoulder will have to be lower than your right. Otherwise you're not going to be in the right position to throw the ball, and your motion will be inhibited. So don't rock back so much that your right shoulder will be *too* low.

COILING YOURSELF

Some compare the early part of the windup with drawing back the bowstring on a crossbow, to get yourself coiled like a spring so that you can uncoil with maximum velocity.

Robin Roberts, the old fireballer and my first roommate, used to think of it as a rocking chair, since you do rock back and are prepared to rock forward. Which brings up a point about your right leg: it's not straight up; it's hinged and coiled, bent at the knee in sort of a rocking-chair position, ready for you to push off on it.

Now, when your left foot is in the air, obviously all your weight is on your right foot. Your head is upright and your body is roughly perpendicular to the ground, not bent over. You can be in a slight crouch, but essentially your body is almost straight up. You may want to tuck in your left shoulder a little bit, but you don't want to hunch over. Your left hip has turned right with your left leg, so that your left shoulder is lined up properly, perpendicular to home plate.

STOP!

Let's stop right here.

When practicing, this is the point in your windup when some experts suggest you should stop and check yourself. The windup is done in a fluid, all-in-one motion, but if you're balanced, you should be able to stop at this point and just stand still. Your pause allows you to get all your weight in balanced position for going to home plate.

In an actual game, this is a point in their delivery where

I take the sign with my bare hand holding the ball in the glove in front of me.

Then my hands go up over my head, my weight shifts to my left foot, which is now back past the rubber, and my right foot pivots toward third base.

My left foot swings around in front of me and up in the air, "kicking" toward third base. My left shoulder aims directly at home plate. My right leg is coiled, ready to push me off in my drive toward the plate.

My hands separate at my waist, and, with my bare hand gripping the ball for the particular pitch I want to throw, I bring my right arm behind me, fully extended but not rigid. My hips are cocked, ready to drive toward the plate. The wrist holding the ball is floppy and cocked in a backward position.

some pitchers feel it's not bad to hesitate slightly, to make sure they're balanced before going to home plate. I don't really recommend it, although I did occasionally do it when I was younger and sometimes had a balance problem, or felt my rhythm was off and my coordination lacking. Sometimes, just to make sure I was in good position, I'd pause and then go toward the plate.

EXPLODE!

At this point in your delivery, your hands separate at your waist, your bare hand gripping the ball for the particular pitch you want to throw. You bring your right arm back behind you, fully extended but not rigid. Your hips are cocked and you're ready to drive toward home plate. As you kick, your right leg comes back into action, coiled for your push-off.

Your movement toward home plate should be an explosion. You get all your weight coiled back on your right foot, and then—boom!—you explode toward home plate with all your momentum and drive in that direction.

In pushing off from the rubber, all your weight should be on the left side of your right foot. The coiled power of your right leg uncoils with powerful thrust, driving your left shoulder at home plate just as your left hip opens toward the plate and your left leg is planted, pointing at the plate.

Your throwing arm will follow, the forearm leading the laid-back, floppy wrist, which is cocked in a backward position. A major thing to remember is that up to the point of release, your wrist should be kept loose and floppy.

Not only do you hold the ball with a fairly loose grip, but your wrist is very relaxed, so free of tension that theoretically someone could slap your hand and the ball would go flying.

Actually, your body is really doing the pitching work for you, until your wrist gets to about your right ear. Then you release the ball with a snap and your arm continues through. With a curve ball you might want to hold on to the ball an instant more, but generally it's about at your right ear that your wrist is cocked and ready to release the ball. Robin Roberts used to say he could almost see himself and hear his wrist popping out in front of him. It's a good concept.

Harvey Haddix used to advise extending your arm as far as you can to try to hand the ball to the catcher.

AIM

Ask most young ball players at whom a pitcher should aim the ball, and they'll probably look at you as if there's something loose upstairs. "At the hitter," they'll say, "of course."

Not so. You're a lot better off if you throw the ball as if you're trying to hand it to the catcher, rather than throwing "off the hitter."

Attempting to hand it to the catcher helps you drive off the mound, because you're trying to reach out. This gets you to throw not only with your arm but with your body as well. Most kids just stand up straight and kind of flip the ball, which puts a lot of strain on the shoulder and elbow. But try to reach out and almost touch the catcher, and you'll really throw the ball.

There's a tendency for young pitchers to look at the hitter and decide, "I'm just going to throw it in an area around home plate between his letters and knees." Well, I find if I concentrate just on the hitter, I usually throw the ball inside, and if he moves off the plate, I throw it even farther inside.

That's one reason Roberto Clemente was one of the toughest hitters to pitch to. He'd stand way in the back of the box, and you'd be afraid you'd throw the ball away if you didn't concentrate on the catcher. If you came inside with the pitch, you'd be afraid it would be like a ball down the middle to him.

Trying to throw the ball right to the catcher and place it in his glove, besides allowing you to drive, also ensures a near-perfect follow-through. You're reaching out and you're in a good position to field the ball.

CONCENTRATION

The best way to concentrate is look at the catcher and concentrate completely on him. Of course, you have to know who the batter is, and work accordingly.

On certain days I have better concentration than I do on others. When I'm pitching well, I can almost visualize what the ball is going to do before I throw it. In other words, I know the particular path it's going to follow all the way to the catcher's glove. The path will be almost exactly the one I want it to take. Everything else is blocked out in my mind, except for the catcher and his glove just sitting there waiting to be hit.

Throughout my delivery I look at the catcher—when my hands are over my head, when my hands are down at my waist, when I kick. Even when my left arm might block my view of him a little bit, I am still looking at the catcher. Then, when the ball is released, I watch the ball all the way.

YOUR FOLLOW-THROUGH

Pitching is a very unorthodox motion. In fact, a number of orthopedic doctors say it's completely unnatural; the natural way to throw is underhand. Just by pitching properly you're putting a lot more stress on your muscles than is natural. So if you have these pitching muscles going in one direction as fast as they possibly can, or with complete tension, and then you suddenly bring them to a halt, it puts even more undue pressure on them. So the object is to release the ball with a fluid motion and let your arm continue until it naturally comes to a stop.

Just as batters or golfers or tennis players don't stop the bat or club or racket at impact, you shouldn't stop your arm at release.

THE IMPORTANCE OF BALANCE

After you release the ball with a snap, your throwing arm should come down to where it almost hits your left knee. Try to get it there, because that will keep you from stopping your arm abruptly, the way so many pitchers do. After releasing the ball, they stop their arm between their waist and chest. Consequently, they don't follow through as they should, and they're not in position to field.

75

Balance is all-important in the windup, especially when your left leg is up in its kick and you're coiled to the right. In practice, stop at this point to check that you are balanced.

If you're not balanced, you may find yourself leaning or falling to your left (A) or to your right (B).

However, if you do make sure your arm comes all the way down to your left knee, you'll be in a balanced position for fielding and throwing.

A good way to assure that you'll be well balanced is to explode your pitch homeward in such a way that your momentum carries your right foot off the rubber and into a position roughly parallel with your left foot, both pointing toward home plate.

Because of his tremendous momentum, Bob Gibson always ends up almost flat on his face. His right leg comes way past his left.

Tom Seaver, who has a very low windup, may brush the mound with his kneecap, but he's an exception. Your left leg should be in an almost completely hinged position, with your thigh and upper leg almost parallel to the ground and your lower leg almost perpendicular to it. Before your right foot comes forward, your left knee is pretty close to the ground. Because your body is extended forward so much as you come through, your right instep (the left side of your right foot) scrapes along the ground when you make your move to home plate.

My philosophy in pitching is to throw away to everybody. In order to get the ball low and away, either to a right-handed or left-handed batter, you *have* to follow through; you can't just stop your arm.

When you're *planning* to follow through properly, you make sure that you're low to the ground. As a result, your legs are hinged and bent, and you're not rigid. This is important because you can't throw very well against a stiff front leg. Throughout your windup, your legs have to be flexible and have some "give" in them.

GLOVE-HAND POSITION

As your left elbow swings around, your glove hand should just naturally reach forward. Then centrifugal force will make it fly out naturally toward home plate, as your left shoulder opens up. Some pitchers consciously fling it into the face of the batter—in other words, as their body comes around to where they'll be facing the plate, they bring the glove around to give the batter something else to look at. I don't do it consciously. It's just something that happens naturally, because if you get in the right position to throw the ball, your left arm has to come from your right to your left. And this means it's going to cross the hitter's line of vision, whether or not you consciously try to do it. Of course, you don't want the glove up in your own face, because that would block out your view of home plate.

Many pitchers finish their delivery with the glove up and open, so they can deflect the ball if it's hit back at them. I don't make a conscious effort to keep it open, but as the glove comes around it's usually in such a position normally that the pocket is looking at home plate.

READINESS TO FIELD

It's obvious that good balance allows you to go right or left, but I think concentration is the most important factor in being ready to field the ball. You have to be watching the ball go to the batter because when he hits it, the sooner you pick it up visually, the better you'll be prepared to react—whether you should get out of the way or deflect it or handle it or cover a base.

I try to land on my toes because I think that helps you

After you release the ball with a snap, your throwing arm should come down to where it almost hits your left knee. Proper follow-through puts you in balanced position to field and throw a ball.

go either way. Being on the balls of your feet gives you pretty good lateral movement either to your right or left. Because I try to get most of my pitches away, especially to right-handed hitters, and because I have a lot of momentum, I have a tendency to fall off a little bit to the left. This puts me at a slight fielding disadvantage. In general, the hardest ball for a right-handed pitcher to field after he's released the ball is to his right, because his momentum is to his left. He gets a little more weight on his left when he comes through because his left is the foot he lands on. When this happens, you almost have to recoil completely and go back to your right.

REVIEWING THE WINDUP

In reviewing the windup, the most important principle to keep in mind is to find your own style, one that affords you good balance, which is essential to effectiveness.

Go over every part of your windup—and work on your balance, especially at the "top" of your windup, when your left leg is up in its kick, and you're coiled to the right. Stop at that point to check it. Once you've mastered balance at that stage, work on a good motion toward home plate. Make sure you're getting back with the weight on your right side when you coil your body. And work on rhythm and coordination throughout your windup.

COMMON DELIVERY FAULTS

There are some common faults in delivery that you should be able to recognize and correct if you're guilty of them.

LANDING HARD

One fault is landing hard, that is, landing on the heel of your left foot instead of the toes or ball of that foot. As you release the ball, you're landing with almost all your weight on your left side, and that left leg has to absorb all the shock. As mentioned earlier, it has to work as sort of a hinge to take all the impact. If it's stiff and doesn't give, not only do you put a lot of pressure on your whole body, but you also rob yourself of any kind of motion.

The jarring effect given by a hard landing will influence the pitch. If in catching a fly ball you run on your heels, the ball will jump all over. The same applies here. So you have to land on the front part of your foot and be moving forward. As your right leg catches up and draws even with it, your left leg has to give a little.

OVERSTRIDING

As you know, your left shoulder has to be lower than your right shoulder when you release the ball. Often, if you stride too far with your left foot you land on your heel, and then you have to reach out so far that your right shoulder can't get into proper position to make the throw.

So stride a distance that's comfortable, below the point

where you feel you're going to do a split. You should land on the ball of your foot, and you have to allow the right side of your body to come across and catch up with your left side.

RUSHING THE DELIVERY

If your body isn't balanced when you rock back on your left foot and then put all your weight back on your right and start to make your turn, you're likely to rush your delivery. In other words, if you come up to the top of your delivery and your weight is not evenly distributed, you may move to the plate without giving your arm time to catch up. As a result, your arm will not be in position to throw the ball and your accuracy is going to be affected. You'll be throwing the pitch too high or too low.

Make sure you're properly balanced and not leaning left or right when you explode toward the plate. That way your arm will come through at the proper time, and your pitches will be where you want them to be.

OVERTHROWING

Overthrowing is trying to throw the ball too hard. Your muscles become very tense; your arm, especially your forearm, becomes rigid, and you don't have the fluidity you want in your delivery. Often when you try to throw very hard, you achieve an effect opposite to what you want. You don't have that floppiness you need in your arm, and the tightening up prevents you from throwing the ball as hard as you want to.

The objective, of course, is to have good rhythm and balance, and to concentrate on the catcher. You want

After you explode toward the plate, your momentum should carry your right foot off the rubber and into a position roughly parallel with your left foot, both pointing home.

Here, I'm off-balance at the end of my delivery, falling off to the left of the mound. As a result, I won't be in good fielding position.

your arm very relaxed, laid behind your body, with your wrist relaxed and floppy, and then cocked to throw as it comes by your ear.

Many times overthrowing will result from being a little tired. Then, instead of letting your natural ability take charge, you try to make up for some of your deficiencies on that particular day by overthrowing.

CROSSING THE CENTER LINE

As I've emphasized, your left shoulder plays a key role in guiding that ball to the plate with the velocity and in the location you want. What guides your left shoulder is your left foot going toward home plate. Your left foot, left hip, and left shoulder are your "chauffeurs" on your drive to the plate.

If your alignment is wrong, then you're going to end up throwing across your body, a very difficult thing to do. In other words, if your left foot lands too much to the right, then your left hip and shoulder are also going to be too much in that direction. And if you're heading right when your target is left or straight ahead, it's going to be very difficult for you to throw a good pitch.

OPENING UP TOO MUCH TO THE LEFT

The same thing is true if you let your foot, hip, and shoulder open up too much to the left. When you're facing home plate, if instead of having them lined up directly toward the plate, you've aligned them perhaps twelve inches to the left, you've opened up so much that you're not driving to the plate with your left shoulder. Your body is swung around to the left, and now all you can do is

With a runner on base, it's usually unwise to go into a full windup. Instead, use a stretch motion, in which you start with both feet pointing toward third, the outside of your right foot in contact with the rubber. Your left shoulder is pointed home, and you grip the ball for the particular pitch with your hands together in front of your body. Pause, look over your left shoulder toward the runner at first, and either throw over there or pitch home.

Here, my right foot is too much on the rubber; I won't be able to push off as I should.

My foot isn't making contact with the rubber at all. You can't legally pitch unless your foot is touching the rubber.

throw with the front of your body, which is no way to make an effective pitch.

STARTING TOO FAR OVER

Another common pitching fault is trying to throw to the outside corner on a right-handed batter, by standing at the far right of the rubber and striding straight forward.

DRAGGING YOUR ARM

When your delivery is going right, your arm starts to come forward naturally when your body starts forward. Yet there are times when you hold your arm back and, all of a sudden, at the top of your delivery—when your left foot is already planted—you realize your body is in position for you to release the ball but your arm is six to eight inches behind. What do you do? You try to throw the ball in a hurry, and it tends to stay up very high.

Throwing the Pitches

L ET'S TALK about how to throw the particular pitches that major-leaguers throw, along with what those pitches are supposed to do and what the dangers are in throwing them.

THE FAST BALL

The fast ball, my favorite, comes in two basic varieties—one that has a tendency to rise as it comes across the plate, and one that has a tendency to sink. To be effective, a fast ball has to move when it crosses the plate.

How the fast ball acts when it comes up to the plate will depend not only on how you grip the ball to throw it, but the type of delivery you employ.

THE RISING FAST BALL
If you're an overhand pitcher and you throw the fast ball

with your middle and index fingers across the big seams and your thumb below, also on the seam, the ball should rise.

The great Sandy Koufax, who threw overhand, had a fast ball that would jump five or six inches, and he'd get a lot of batters to hit fly balls. Nolan Ryan throws the same way; his ball really rises.

If you're a three-quarter pitcher, your fast ball will sort of tail up a little bit and come back in to a right-handed batter, and if you're a right-handed sidearm hurler, the ball will move from left to right.

The reason the ball tends to rise when you throw it this way is that your fingertips are putting pressure on the seams; as the ball leaves your hand you're pulling down and giving it a backward rotation.

THE SINKING FAST BALL

If you place your middle and index fingers on top of the ball where the seams are closest together, and your thumb on the bottom, the ball should sink if it is kept down. Re-

When you grip the fast ball across the seams—index and middle fingers on top, thumb on the bottom—the pitch should rise as it crosses the plate.

Grip the ball with your middle and index fingers on top of the ball, where the seams are closest together, and with your thumb on the bottom, and if it is kept down, the fast ball should sink.

member, to throw this sinking fastball, your middle and index fingers should each be on one of the narrow seams and in the same direction as the seams (not across them).

It's possible to turn your wrist over a little more and thereby turn the ball over, the rotation making the ball drop down even more. But that can hurt your elbow, so avoid it.

THROWING THE FAST BALL

In throwing either type of fast ball overhand, your wrist is laid back and, as the ball is released, is flipped toward home plate, with your hand perpendicular to the ground.

Throwing three-quarters, your hand would be coming from, say, between ten and eleven o'clock, and sidearm from nine o'clock. In the sidearm delivery, your fingers would be parallel to the ground.

THE SPEED OF THE FAST BALL

Good major-league fast balls have been clocked at speeds approaching 100 miles per hour. How fast you can expect *your* fast ball to be will depend on several factors: how hard you throw (which is dictated mainly by your natural ability), your experience, and what kind of stuff you have on a particular day.

Often, if you have good control, you don't have to throw as hard as you might when control is lacking and you're trying to overpower the hitters or at least to put a little extra on the ball. I know there have been times when I've been able to breeze through a game, when I've been able to make good pitches without having to throw very hard. And I've also experienced games in which I've had to rely more on my stuff and throw harder to compensate for an off day in control. When you're in the kind of situation where you've got to get more from your fast ball, remember that it's important not to tense up. I make sure I pitch within my limits—I try to throw with perhaps 90 percent of my power.

THE ADVANTAGE OF THE FAST BALL ...

Gene Woodling, who was a fine hitter with the New York Yankees, feels that a good fast ball is the best pitch in baseball from the pitcher's standpoint.

I agree, and so, I think, would fast-ball pitchers like Tom Seaver and Nolan Ryan. You can make a mistake with a good fast ball and get away with it, whereas you're not likely to be that lucky making one on another type of pitch. For instance, a slider is good in only one or possibly two areas—but you can make a mistake and throw a fast ball down the middle of the plate, and *if it moves,* the hitter might pop it up or line it out.

... AND ITS DANGERS

The big danger with a fast ball is throwing it down the middle of the plate without much movement on it, and not throwing it well; that's why I rarely just try to throw it past the hitter. I try to throw it to a spot, not necessarily an exact spot, but some place within either the inner half or outer half of the plate.

What a fast-ball pitcher can't ever forget is that a fast ball is the easiest pitch to hit out of the park, especially if it's up in the strike zone (unless, of course, you're facing a low-ball hitter). Throwing the ball poorly, in the hitter's power zone with nothing on it, is obviously one of the big problems confronting a fast-ball pitcher.

Another hazard is getting behind the hitter, which spoils the effectiveness of your fast ball. If you're ahead of the batter, he has to look for the breaking ball. But if he's ahead of you, he knows you've got to come in with a fast ball—and wham! One of the worst things that can befall a fast-ball pitcher is for him to be behind the hitters all day, so they're able to gauge the speed of his fast ball.

WHERE TO THROW IT

Where a fast ball is most effective depends on what kind of fast-ball pitcher you are. If you're a sinker-ball pitcher, obviously you're most effective if you keep your fast ball low in the strike zone. Because the ball is sinking, the batter is likely to hit the fast ball on the ground.

A fast-ball pitcher like myself, however, is best off keeping the ball up and in or low and away. Actually, even when I keep the ball down and in, it's a pretty good pitch, and the velocity is good on the outside of the plate, too.

In general, down and away is the preferable place to throw a fast ball. It's a much better pitch than a ball that's up, which is probably going to be hit for a fly ball. If the batter strokes that fly ball pretty well, sometimes he'll hit a home run. (There are a few exceptions—say a low curve ball thrown by a right-handed pitcher to a left-handed hitter. But that fly ball will normally stay in the park.)

A hitter will see a fast ball up in his eyes better than he will a low ball. But, ironically, he'll often be deceived by it because he *thinks* he sees it better than he actually does. The reason for this is the movement the ball has on it.

Sandy Koufax had a hop on his fast ball, and I think mine and Nolan Ryan's do, too. As a result of being deceived, the batter will aim at where he thinks he'll be hitting it squarely, but because of the hop he'll actually make contact with the bottom of the ball, and hit it up in the air.

THE CURVE BALL

OKAY TO THROW ONE?

The jury is still out on whether it's harmful for a young player to start throwing a curve ball before a certain age. I don't think it's really been medically proven either way whether or not you're likely to develop "Little League elbow" or some such ailment if you start throwing curves too young. I threw curve balls at a relatively early age and did experience some arm problems, but none with the elbow. True, a curve ball does put more stress on your arm than other pitches, but if you learn to throw it properly, under the proper guidance of a qualified coach, it shouldn't harm you. As with a fast ball or any other pitch, you've got to remember not to stop your arm abruptly during delivery, or your arm or shoulder is going to be hurt.

The key then is proper coaching, combined with your attitude and learning ability. If it's decided you should wait a year or more before you start throwing curves, abide by the decision.

In any case, eventually you're going to have to learn how to throw one, so let's discuss it.

93

THE GRIP

The grip for throwing a curve ball can vary. For instance, I hold mine almost the same way I do for a fast ball, except that I rotate the ball a little to the right so that more of the side seam is showing. Also, as you can see in the photo, my thumb is at an angle to the seams.

A curve ball can also be thrown with your fingers across the narrow seams.

For the fast ball I hold the ball out on the tips of my fingers, but for the curve ball I find it more comfortable to move the ball back as I grip it. But even though you hold it farther back in your hand, there should still be a little daylight between the ball and the flesh between your thumb and index finger.

In releasing the fast ball, you'll remember, the middle and index fingers applied the main pressure, aided by the thumb. To throw the curve ball, you grip the ball with the

The grip for throwing a curve ball can vary. I hold mine almost the same way I do for a fast ball, except that I rotate the ball a little to the right so that more of the side seam is showing. My thumb is at an angle to the seams. In delivering the curve ball, your hand should be up and turned to the side so your fingertips are holding the ball, your palm toward your ear. The ball is held farther back in your hand than for a fast ball, but there should still be some daylight.

same fingers, but the pressure at release is mainly on the padded end of the middle finger and the right side, the fleshy part, of both joints of the thumb.

Whichever way you grip the ball, the pressure is on the middle finger when you release it. Your index finger is essentially a guide. Sandy Koufax hardly ever used his index finger at all, but most people need to, unless they have exceptionally large hands and can get their fingers almost all the way around the ball.

THE DELIVERY

You deliver the curve ball differently than you do the fast ball. Instead of your wrist being laid back as your arm comes through, your hand should be up and turned to the side so your fingertips are holding the ball, your palm toward your ear.

Unlike the delivery of the fast ball, in throwing a curve your elbow is out in front of your lower arm, leading the way. Then the forearm comes down at a right angle, and as you release the ball, you pull down with your thumb and the ball snaps off the right side of your middle finger. The spin on a curve ball is *toward* the plate (as opposed to the backward rotation of the fast ball). The feeling I always want to have in releasing the ball is my elbow out in front of me and then snapping the ball— almost so that I hear it—with my arm moving smoothly from my ear toward my waist.

PROPERTIES OF THE CURVE BALL

A curve ball should actually curve—move from the plane it was traveling along when it first left your hand.

Not many pitchers have "pure" curve balls. The flight

of your curve ball will depend on the position you throw it from. If you pitch overhand, it will probably just break straight down. If you're a right-hander who throws from a three-quarter position, the curve ball will move from right to left—*and* drop as it reaches the plate. If you throw it sidearm, as a right-hander against a right-handed batter, it will just move in a flat plane from right to left; very seldom will it drop as well.

BREAKING AND SPEED

A good curve ball will break from its path about two-thirds of the way from the pitcher. How much it will break depends on such factors as where it's thrown from, how fast it's thrown, the release, and the tightness of the spin.

If you throw the curve overhand, the ball may start out looking as if it's over the batter's head and then drop as much as five or six *feet* to below his knees as it crosses the plate.

From a three-quarter delivery, where you're a little on top, your curve ball has a slight chance of breaking down. But a slow curve ball pitched sidearm has no such chance, because the position of your hands makes it spin in a flat arc sideward.

Your curve ball's speed, which you can—and probably should—vary throughout the game, is a big factor in determining how much the ball breaks. The harder you throw it, the less it will break. This has the advantage of making it easier to get in the strike zone, but the disadvantage of making it easier for the batter to hit. A slow curve, too, unless it's thrown *really* slow, and has a chance to both drop and curve through the strike zone, doesn't usually pose too much challenge for the hitter either.

(Incidentally, whether or not I try to get the curve ball in the strike zone will vary with the situation. When I start a hitter off with a 0–0 count, I do want to throw the curve for a strike. But with two strikes on him, I probably just want him to chase the ball, so I'll make sure to keep the curve low, rather than worry about it's being in the strike zone.)

WHERE TO THROW A CURVE

If you're a right-handed pitcher, avoid throwing a ball down and in to a left-handed hitter, because for some reason most lefties are good low-ball hitters. Against a righty hitter, though, a low curve is a good pitch. (Against a right-handed hitter, I try to throw the curve at the catcher's left shoulder.)

The one that gets hit pretty hard is the hanging curve ball, the one whose spin isn't as tight as it should be, and that stays up in the strike zone.

BREAKING AND THE TIGHT SPIN

As mentioned earlier, how much your curve ball breaks will also depend on how tight you make the spin on the ball.

The best curve ball is one that the good hitter can't recognize when it leaves the pitcher's hand. It looks like a fast ball, and suddenly it breaks. The hard-to-identify curve ball is the one with the tightest spin, and that comes with friction from the tightness of the release. To accomplish this you need a strong grip on the ball, but you don't want your muscles so tense that your wrist lacks fluidity and won't bend.

DANGEROUS CURVES

The danger in throwing a curve ball is that, if thrown improperly, it will rotate loosely and just hang over the plate, hardly breaking. A hanging curve ball is one pitch that hitters feast on, so make that ball break.

A common problem is a pitcher throwing a curve when his arm isn't yet in the proper position. In other words, instead of releasing the ball in front of him, he'll throw from way back, with his elbow still leading the way. When you do it like that, your left shoulder is up and you never have a chance of getting the ball down properly.

LEARNING TO THROW A CURVE

A good way to learn to throw a curve ball is to stand with your legs parallel and slightly apart and just keep throwing the ball, almost as if you're throwing darts. They teach it that way at Arizona State (where I studied a year and a half before going on to Towson State in Maryland), and at the University of Southern California.

Then, once you get that motion perfected, it's a relatively easy matter to let your elbow lead the way and work on the spin, and then work the whole thing in with your windup.

THE SLIDER

The slider is possibly the most important pitch you can have in your arsenal. Its revolutionary effect on modern baseball is reflected in the lower batting averages of today compared with those in the years before the slider came into use.

A slider should look like a fast ball and behave something like a curve—that is, suddenly break down and maybe five or six inches to the left (in the case of a right-handed pitcher throwing to a right-handed batter). Mel Stottlemyre, who uses a three-quarter delivery, has a good slider and is very tough on right-handed hitters.

The type of delivery will affect how much the main break of the slider is likely to be.

RESEMBLANCE TO THE FAST BALL

What makes the slider resemble the fast ball is the tightness of its spin (as opposed to the curve ball, whose spin a good hitter can sometimes pick up and identify). They say a good slider becomes a spinning dot, a fast, tight corkscrew action.

If that dot isn't tight—if it's a big dot coming up to the batter—watch out. That's going to be a *hanging* slider, which is probably the worst pitch in baseball from the pitcher's point of view.

But on the good side: a slider's resemblance to a fast ball makes it difficult for the hitter to identify it—and a slider is easier to throw in the strike zone than a curve, because the slider doesn't break as much.

THE GRIP

Generally, I hold the ball the same way for a slider that I do for the fast ball—index and middle fingers across the wide seams and the thumb below. But when I grip the ball for the slider, I turn it about the same amount as I do the curve ball, and hold it a little to the right of center (which isn't as drastic a change as you might think).

The grip for a slider is in between fast ball and curve,

I generally hold the ball for a slider the same way that I do for the fast ball—index and middle fingers across the wide seams, and the thumb below. But when I grip it, I turn it about the same amount as I do for the curve ball, and hold it a little to the right of center. A slider isn't held quite at the fingertips the way a fast ball is, but neither is it choked the way a curve ball is.

too. It's held not quite at the tips of your fingers the way a fast ball is, but neither is it choked the way a curve ball is.

THROWING THE SLIDER

When I throw the slider, I try to think fast ball all the way, although there are some differences.

The motion for throwing a slider is somewhere in between the motion for a fast ball and for a curve. You do lay your wrist back, just as you do with the fast ball, but instead of having your wrist come straight forward, you cut it a little, and actually throw it with your wrist. I think throwing with the wrist is the best way, although there are those who recommend an arm motion where you bring your wrist over straight forward and your elbow across your body. But that method puts tremendous strain on both your shoulder and elbow.

So as you come through in your delivery, don't have your wrist laid back and then come straight, with the pressure on the side of the ball. Instead, put a lot of pressure on your middle finger—more than you do in throwing the curve—and throw the baseball almost as you would a football, making sure your wrist stays on top and doesn't go off to the side. (It should be above your forearm, facing straight on to the plate.) And don't drop your arm.

When you throw the slider, your index and middle fingers should point to where you're throwing. I put a fair amount of pressure on both fingers, slightly more on my middle one.

DANGER OF THE SLIDER

If a slider breaks sharply, it's usually in a good spot. But if it doesn't break as it should and just sort of hangs there, the hitter is right on it, and if it's up in the strike zone, he's going to pull it.

WHERE TO THROW THE SLIDER

A slider is a very effective pitch, but normally only when it's low and away. Because its velocity is less than that of a fast ball, it's better that it not be thrown over the middle of the plate, where it will usually be hit pretty hard. It might be effective right at the batter, breaking over the inside corner, but best of all is a slider that moves away from the hitter.

THE CHANGE-UP

I'm often asked how many pitches a pitcher needs to be good. Unless you're an overpowering pitcher like Nolan Ryan, you probably need three or four different pitches to be successful.

I think an essential part of any pitcher's repertoire or assortment of pitches is the change-up. Also known as the "change-of-pace," or simply the "change," it's an often misunderstood pitch.

Many people think that the only thing that will fool a hitter on a change is a change in speed—and so the only thing you should be concerned with is slowing down the velocity of the pitch. I used to think that way when I was in high school, but it's not so.

A prime object in pitching is to throw every pitch so it looks the same, so you seem to be using the very same motion, and so the velocity of your arm coming through neither speeds up nor slows down.

If you throw the ball at a slower speed, but your arm action is different, it will tip off the batter that a change-up is coming. So make that motion the same.

THE AIM OF THE CHANGE-UP
The lower you get the change-up in the strike zone, the more effective it's likely to be.

THE GRIP
To throw a change-up, grip the ball with either two or three fingers on top, whichever is most comfortable. (I

Some pitchers prefer to throw a change-up with two fingers on top (A), *but I prefer three* (B, C). *Either way, to throw a change-up, put the ball as far back in your hand as possible, so there's no daylight between the ball and the skin between your thumb and index finger. Because the ball is so far back in your hand, most of the pressure will be on the knuckles (rather than the fingertips, as it is with a fast ball) and this will prevent the ball from traveling very fast.*

prefer three.) Put the ball as far back in your hand as possible, which is called "choking" the ball. With this grip, you don't see daylight between the ball and the skin between your thumb and index finger.

Grasp the ball almost as you would for your fast ball, except that, instead of the pressure being on the tips of your fingers, most of the pressure will be on your knuckles, because the ball is so far back in your hand.

THE DELIVERY

Having the ball that far back makes your wrist more passive than it would be normally. As a result, even though you try to throw the ball as hard as possible, it won't travel very fast or hard. And this little difference—the fact that it's slower than the fast ball, while the delivery makes the batter get set for a fast ball—is enough to make the pitch effective.

Some hurlers, ever mindful that the pitch should be relatively slow, mistakenly try to throw with a slower motion. But because most hitters concentrate on the pitcher's hand at the point of release, they'll know something off speed is coming if your arm slows way down before you release the ball. Anyway, slowing your arm movement really isn't necessary, because holding the ball back in your hand will prevent it from coming in very fast. So make sure your arm speed is the same when you throw the change as when you throw the fast ball.

THE NATURAL WAY TO THROW

I've found that holding the ball with three fingers, well back in my hand, is a natural way of throwing the ball.

I like to twist my wrist a little to the left just as I'm

releasing the ball, to give it kind of a screwball motion. This does two things: (1) it makes the ball twist away from left-handed batters or into right-handers, and (2) it allows me to hang on to the ball and follow through with my arm. That last point is important, because many pitchers, when throwing a change-up, tend to stop their motion short as soon as they release the ball. If you turn your wrist a little to the left as you release, as I do, you'll make sure that your arm follows through.

Stu Miller, who probably had one of the best changes of all times, compared his motion to pulling down a window shade. In other words, your wrist doesn't snap as it comes through, but instead remains rather stiff.

That's a good comparison to keep in mind. When you're throwing a change, lay your wrist back as you would for a fast ball, then pull down that imaginary window shade and you'll have the desired effect.

CHANGE-UP SPEEDS

It's possible to vary the speeds of a change-up pitch, but the main thing is not to telegraph to the batter that a change is coming. If you throw it too slow, it will give the batter what amounts to a second chance to hit. What I mean is, if he had made his stride, preparing for a fast ball, a pitch that's very slow might give him time to recoil his hips and shoulders, cock his bat again, and hit the ball. On the other hand, if your change-up is too fast, the way the hitter reacts—by hitting the ball—will let you know it's too fast.

USING THE CHANGE

A change-up's effectiveness depends on a sense of comparison. But until a hitter has seen your fast ball and how hard you're throwing it, he's not going to have anything to compare with—and get fooled by. So it's not likely you'd throw him a change-up on the game's first pitch to him. But you might use a change on a first pitch to him on a later at-bat, once he's seen your fast ball and is expecting it. It's very satisfying to watch him get set for the fast ball, get his body way out in front—and then realize you've fooled him with a change-up.

DANGER OF THE CHANGE-UP
The biggest danger is letting the hitter know that a change-up is coming, because then he has a chance to get set and adjust his timing. And if the ball is up in the strike zone, it's probably a pitch he can pull.

ADVANTAGE OF THE CHANGE
I think a change-up (with its resemblance to a fast ball) is especially effective for a fast-ball pitcher who doesn't throw many breaking balls over the plate. At this point in my career, I do have four good pitches—fast ball, curve, slider, and change—but I don't get my curve over the plate as often as I'd like. As a fast-ball pitcher, I'll get into situations where hitters are looking for fast balls and I can really fool them for easy outs with my change. For me, a change-up is a little bit easier to throw over the plate than a curve because it doesn't break as much.

THE BEST PLACE TO THROW A CHANGE
Keep your change down in the strike zone as much as possible. The reason for this is that normally a hitter will be fooled by it, and the chances of hitting a low pitch

level for a line drive are less than on a ball that fools him at his eyes.

NOVELTY PITCHES

There are numerous other pitches in use today, many in the "novelty" category and not all worth studying. The worthwhile ones should await your attention until you've mastered the other, more basic ones.

THE KNUCKLE BALL

A rather revolutionary pitch is the knuckle ball, which is thrown with your fingertips dug into the rounded part of the fat seams.

The ball is delivered with a stiff wrist, and when it leaves your hand it has no rotation, which allows the air to affect it—aerodynamically move it.

Advantage. It doesn't put a lot of stress on the arm

The knuckle ball is thrown with the fingertips of your middle and index fingers dug into the rounded part of the fat seams. Deliver the ball with a stiff wrist, and as it leaves your hand, it will have no rotation.

because it doesn't take maximum effort to throw. Wilbur Wood, one of the pitchers who have been exceptionally successful with it, has been able to start both ends of a double-header.

Disadvantage. I don't think it's a very good pitch to throw because you throw it with a different motion than you use for other pitches. Your motion is a giveaway, and batters will tend to take the pitch if the count on them permits.

Also, it's a hard pitch to throw. I used to experiment in high school, throwing a knuckler with a sidearm motion if I was way ahead of the count. But it never did for me what it did for Wood or for Hoyt Wilhelm or somebody like that.

You know things are not going too well when the manager suggests that you go to work on a knuckle ball.

Before Wilbur Wood began specializing on the knuckler, he had pretty good "normal" stuff—a curve, fast ball and so forth—and he just started to throw the knuckler. He played a number of years with Hoyt Wilhelm, which certainly didn't hurt him or his knuckle ball any.

THE SPITBALL

There's been so much talk about spitballs in recent seasons, we ought to say a couple of words about them.

I've never thrown a spitter in a game, although I've experimented with it. You throw it by putting a little moisture on the end of your fingers and holding the ball on the slick part instead of on the seam.

It's kind of hazardous to your arm because, instead of the ball being released at the end of a normal delivery, at the point you know it's going to be released, it sort of *slips* out of your hand, sometimes sooner than you expect.

So I don't recommend it, and I wouldn't want to see it legalized. As it is, hitters have enough problems, or so it seems from the way they've been legislating against pitchers—lowering the mounds, bringing in the fences, livening up the ball, and coming up with a designated-hitter rule. Yes, there are pitchers who use it, but leave the illegal spitter to those few veterans, and spend your time concentrating on legitimate pitches.

Control

OVERALL, I THINK good control—pitching the ball where you want it—is the most important ingredient of successful pitching. It will often make up for lack of good stuff, or will make your stuff effective.

There aren't that many overpowering pitchers who can succeed on great stuff alone. Many a pitcher with outstanding stuff isn't able to pitch particularly well because he can't throw the ball in the right area. And if he throws hard enough, often enough, in the middle of the plate, he's going to get hurt.

On many occasions I've had great stuff and lost. Other times I didn't—and won. Usually the difference between winning and losing those games was control. One in which I had both good stuff and good control was a twelve-inning game in Boston that I consider one of the best I've pitched in my whole career. In the first inning, I was throwing everything down the middle of the plate and they were crushing the pitches down the left-field line. Luckily, most of those line drives were either fouls or outs. Then, for the next eleven innings, the pitches I made were perfect; the stuff I had was consistent throughout the game.

A memorable game for me was the sixth game of the 1971 World Series. I didn't have very good stuff, but I had excellent control, and my manager felt it was a much better pitched game than the one earlier in that Series when I'd struck out a bunch of hitters.

When you've consistently got both good stuff and good control, you're a super pitcher. Sandy Koufax was that. Robin Roberts had both qualities, and so did Warren Spahn. Among active pitchers, Dave McNally and Bob Gibson have both. Whitey Ford didn't have an outstanding fast ball, but he had great breaking stuff and he could make good pitches.

DEVELOPING CONTROL

Can you develop control? Definitely. By practice and concentration.

Make sure that whenever you throw a ball, even on the sidelines, you throw to a particular place, eventually a corner. Try to make every pitch have a purpose. That's one of the basic principles of pitching. You don't just throw the ball, you throw to an area. Obviously, you're not always going to be successful, but if you have an idea of what you're trying to do with a pitch and where you're trying to throw the ball, it will improve your ability to do it.

You can't expect to have pinpoint control—that is, the

ability to throw to a precise spot—right away. You should start out just learning to throw the ball over the plate. Than, as you mature, your coordination matures. Your motor skills become a little more refined, and when they advance, you can start aiming, not just to get the ball over the plate in the strike zone, but over the inside corner or outside corner, high, low, and so forth.

When you learn to play golf, you first learn to hit the ball to the green. Then, after you've started getting it there all the time, you start hitting for the pin. It's the same thing in pitching. Start by getting it over the plate, and, when you get into the groove and you know you can get the ball in a certain generalized area regularly, then you go for the inside half or outside half, the inside or outside corner.

WHEN YOUR GOOD CONTROL IS MISSING

You may have good control most of the time, but not have it in a given game. If so, you can look for quite a few things (besides a lot of runs by the opposing team).

First of all, ask yourself whether you are concentrating, whether you are picking up the catcher. Is he giving you a good target and are you concentrating on that? Are you throwing off the batter instead of to the catcher?

Then check out such items as whether you're balanced at the top of your windup.

Is your foot going straight toward home plate? Is your arm in the right position?

Be sure you're throwing with your natural delivery,

and not dropping down to make a certain pitch so your arm is not in its normal position.

Are you striding correctly? If you're throwing the ball a little too low, maybe you should take a bigger stride. If you're up in the strike zone, you should probably shorten your stride.

I mentioned earlier that I used to draw a line with my heel from the middle of the rubber toward home plate. I made sure that my left foot landed on the left side of the line and, obviously, that my right foot went on the right side of the line. The footprints also showed me where my stride was and whether I was landing in the same spot. Today when I warm up, I still try to step in the same place. (The best time to work on your pitching is not during a game, but when you're throwing on the sidelines; then you can work on the direction of your foot and your stride.) I check whether my footprints are in the same place. And even in a game, I'll check those prints to make sure I'm not throwing across my body.

IMPROVING YOUR CONTROL

Think you have trouble with control? My first two years in the majors I walked 130 men in the same number of innings. There were several reasons for this. First of all, my windup was inconsistent. My kick wasn't the same each time, and my balance was off. I cut my windup down, from a real high kick to one where my knee was a little above my waist. And my control came around.

The way prize fighters do shadowboxing, I'd frequently go out on the mound and do a shadow windup—go through my windup without a ball. I'd go into my motion, rock back and turn my hips, check my balance, and make sure that I had my knee only as high as I wanted it to be. Then I'd pretend to be releasing the ball and follow through.

Probably the most important thing I did to improve my control, though, was work on my concentration. When I'd throw on the sidelines, I'd have the catcher sit on the outside corner as if I were throwing to a right-handed batter, and I'd make sure I tried to throw the ball there. Whether I got it high or low wasn't especially important —as long as I threw it *away* from the batter. When you throw the ball away to the batter, you have to follow through. You have to make sure that you're coming through and going right to the catcher. And most important, you have to concentrate. As a result of doing this, I released the ball when I knew my body was in the right position. It helped my control tremendously.

WHEN PITCHES GO WRONG

When pitches go where you don't want them to, there's usually a particular reason for them being too high, too low, too far inside, or too far outside.

A PITCH TOO HIGH
Often the key cause of this problem is that your left shoulder is above your right shoulder when you release the ball. This often comes from landing on your heel rather than your toes, so you can't get your shoulder back down where it should be. Land on your left heel, and

your body's likely to be at a 45-degree angle instead of being level. Another cause can be that you're dragging your arm—having your body in position and throwing the ball before your arm is ready.

By the way, I normally keep the ball up, even though when I first came to the majors, Hank Bauer, who was then the Orioles' manager, said, "You can't pitch high in this league." Then one game I came in in relief and walked the first two men on eight pitches, seven of which bounced in the dirt. Hank came running out to the mound shouting, "I didn't mean you. You *can* pitch high."

They used to say that Sandy Koufax couldn't pitch high in the National League because of its low strike zone. Yet he set all kinds of strikeout records and had a low earned run average almost every year.

A PITCH TOO LOW

Having your arm out in front of your body will result in a pitch being too low. Your arm will be ready to throw the ball before your left foot lands, so you throw the ball with no way to get your body behind the throw, and usually the ball goes on or close to the plate.

Understriding can also cause a low pitch. If you don't take a big enough stride, your foot will touch down way before it's supposed to. Then your arm is already through and you're not in proper position to throw the ball.

A PITCH OUTSIDE TO A RIGHTY

Outside pitches usually come from opening up too much. If you throw the ball correctly, you have your left shoulder pointing where you want to throw, just as an infielder or outfielder will. But if you get your hips so far out of the correct path that your left shoulder is pointing too much to the left—instead of straight at the plate—to the left is where you're going to throw the ball.

A PITCH INSIDE

Throwing too far inside usually results from throwing across your body. This will often happen when you drive toward home plate and, instead of opening up and getting square with the plate, you turn your foot toward the batter and your body follows. Also, frequently when you throw inside, you're throwing off the hitter, instead of to the catcher.

INSIDE—AND TOO FAR INSIDE

I think there definitely is a place in baseball for pitching inside and outside. Obviously, if you've been pitching a batter away all the time and he moves up on the plate, you have to keep him honest, you have to throw the ball inside. Otherwise, he moves up on the plate looking for a ball away, and if you give him what he expects, he'll be able to hit that ball more easily. So you know you're going to have to move him off the plate, and the way you accomplish that is to pitch inside.

But before you try it, you have to take into consideration what kind of control you have. When you pitch inside, is the ball going to miss the plate by a foot inside? If it is, it's going to hit the batter. But if you can come inside within four or five inches of the plate, then go ahead and do it. It depends on how much pitching skill you have, how fine your control is. I know I can try to throw a ball ten inches inside and it's going to be in that neighborhood.

It wasn't always that way. As a young pitcher, I sometimes had the tendency to virtually close my eyes and pitch the ball as hard as I could. I did this in the state finals in Phoenix Municipal Park in Arizona with a Babe Ruth League team (I'd previously played Little League and Pony League ball) and hit a batsman with a sidearm pitch.

The umpire came out to the mound and warned me, "If you throw another pitch sidearm and hit a batter, we're going to disqualify you from the tournament." Whether or not it would have been legal for him to do it, I deserved to be jumped on. I was throwing too hard, I wasn't looking where I was throwing the ball, and I was pitching with a different delivery from the one that was normal to me. If the umpire knew I'd closed my eyes when I pitched, I don't think he would have been amused. Certainly the batter I hit didn't think it was funny.

I don't believe in throwing at a batter intentionally, even though I believe I can hit a batter anytime I want to, and batters have the responsibility of getting out of the way. The plate and the "air rights" over it belong to the pitcher.

Unfortunately, a lot of hitters have the habit of moving into the ball. They stand either deep in the box or even with the plate, and then they lunge into the ball. If the ball tails and goes into this type of hitter, it's very difficult for him to get out of the way. Tony Conigliaro, who suffered a shattering eye injury, is a perfect example. He'd stand right on the plate and stay there as the pitch came in. I've hit Bill Freehan with pitches I thought were strikes because he goes into the ball so much.

From a pitcher's standpoint, a hitter who stands over the plate looks very menacing, so you have to pitch inside. But not to hit him. Remember, the ball is a lethal weapon and the batter is not anticipating that the ball is going to be thrown at him.

The only time a pitcher is ever justified in throwing at an opposing hitter is if the opposing pitcher has been throwing at his team's hitters. I've been involved in that sort of thing only once. I threw the ball between Gary Peters' legs after he'd been throwing at our hitters. You have to protect your hitters this way, because if the other pitcher is going to have license to throw at your teammates, it definitely will affect their ability to hit. Being thrown at is something that frightens, or at least bothers, most hitters. But other than to protect your own hitters, there's no reason to throw at a batter. Even if you're getting roughed up by their good hitting, or if you're just not performing well, it's not sufficient cause to throw at the hitters. Remember, if you strike them out, they don't throw a bat at you.

WILD PITCHES

Loss of control shows up most dramatically in wild pitches.

Wild pitches can be caused by bad catchers, but almost always it's the fault of the pitcher. If you're a breaking-ball pitcher, it's easy to throw a lot of wild pitches. This is true especially if you're throwing a lot of balls in the dirt, because when a breaking ball hits the dirt, its spin makes it more difficult to catch. Tremendous velocity on your pitches can also cause wild pitches. One season I led the Northern League in wild pitches, for several reasons: I was wild, I was inexperienced, and the catcher wasn't as skillful as I was to find catchers to be in higher-classification ball.

If you're throwing wild pitches, it's probably due to a lack of concentration. If you're throwing the ball where the catcher can't catch it, possibly you're not throwing the ball at the catcher.

It seems so simple to look at the catcher and throw the ball there, but it's hard. Golfers are told to watch the ball all the way, but very few do. And very few tennis players really see the racket hit the ball, even though they should. The same sort of thing seems to happen in baseball. You look at the catcher, all right, but you're so intent on throwing the ball hard you take your eyes off your target for a moment. The catcher gives you a target, which is in the middle of an area bounded by his knees and shoulders. If you can throw the ball in that area, the catcher should catch it. If you're getting it in there and he's not catching it, then it's his fault. But overall it's a matter of your failure to concentrate totally.

So if you're having trouble with wildness, do your best to concentrate on getting the ball into that zone. That's how I like to pitch. I've walked a lot of players in my career, but I was never wild to the inside or outside—just up or down. And it was simply a matter of getting my rhythm straightened out and perfecting my windup so that it was more consistent.

WALKS

When you talk about a pitcher's wildness, usually you're not referring to wild pitches but to the great number of walks he gives up.

Walks don't always necessarily mean wildness. There are some games when you're just a little bit off; you're trying to make good pitches but miss by just a few inches and end up walking the batter. And there will be some ball games when you don't have excellent control and you'll be trying to pitch a little bit too fine, so that instead of giving a man a good pitch to hit, you'll just try to make the pitch in a good spot and end up walking him. And sometimes, in certain parks, you may have the bases open and particular hitters you don't want to pitch to, and you end up walking them.

In general, though, a lot of walks *does* mean you're wild.

My philosophy has been that with a good defense behind me I'd rather have the hitter hit the ball and possibly become an out, than let him become a sure base runner with a walk. When I'm not making him hit the ball, I'm not doing my job and not helping the ball club.

CAUSES OF WALKS

Probably the most significant mistake pitchers make is to get behind the hitter. The main cause of this is failing to concentrate fully on the first pitch.

Often, getting behind the hitter is something that comes

from being defensive, not having the confidence in your ability to get the hitter out and so trying to trick him rather than challenge him.

Keep in mind that a hitter who is having a good year at the plate is going to get a hit only about three times out of every ten at-bats. That's when he's having a good year! If he's not having a good year, you're going to get him out fourteen or fifteen times out of twenty at-bats.

If you're defensive in your pitching, you tend to become too fine and, as a result, you throw the first pitch or two for balls. Now you're behind the count, and you've either got to come in with the pitch that the hitter is looking for, or take a chance on missing the strike zone and walking him.

So try to stay ahead of the hitters. Work on your control and get into a groove where you can really concentrate on your catcher. Try to be like good major-league pitchers who emphasize getting the ball over the plate, first, and with something on it, second—instead of throwing the ball with something on it and *then* concentrating on getting it over the plate.

IT HELPS TO PITCH REGULARLY

Pitching in regular rotation should help your control. I know that at the beginning of the season my control is somewhat off because I don't pitch as regularly as I do in June, July, and August.

You can also help your control in between starts by concentrating and working on the different pitches you're going to use in your next game. Say we're going to Boston and I know I'm going to have to get my curve ball over, and that I'm going to have to use my slider, and that they don't hit the change-up very well. Then I'll make sure I work on those pitches in preparation for my start.

WHEN YOU'RE BEHIND THE COUNT

Control shouldn't be a problem if you manage to stay ahead of the hitters but, of course, that's easier said than done. How can you avoid walks when you get behind the hitter? One way is not to be afraid to come in with a pitch. If you have good stuff and good ability, you can risk challenging the hitters. It comes down to a matter of: "You know what's coming—can you hit it?"

For instance, the 2–0 pitch is crucial because a batter is almost certain that a fast ball is coming, and he gets set for it. But I've found in batting practice that if you throw a hitter ten fast balls—and he knows they're coming—if you throw them well, he's still going to have trouble hitting more than two or three solidly.

So when you're behind the hitter, 2–0, you have an option: throw the fast ball the hitter is expecting, or, if you have confidence you can get your breaking ball over, throw your breaking ball. It's a good time to throw it, because hitters are usually looking for the fast ball in that sort of situation. They want to make sure they get a good pitch to hit, one they can get a good swing at. Be careful, though, not to stay in the same pattern. If you *always* come across with a breaking ball on 2–0, the hitters will be looking for it, and so good-bye surprise element—and maybe good-bye ball, as well. Of course, as I've mentioned, if you make good pitches, if you throw low-and-away sliders, or low-and-away fast balls, they're still going to be tough pitches to hit, even if the batter expects it.

If you throw it in the middle of the plate, though—

and on 2–0 your main concern is to get the ball some-where in the strike zone—it could be trouble for you. For instance, as a fast-ball pitcher, if I throw a breaking ball on a 2–0 count, all I do is worry about getting it over. The same applies on my first pitch to a batter. Normally he's expecting a fast ball, and if I throw a breaking ball, it's just fine if I get it over *anywhere*.

And I'm not afraid to groove a 3–0 pitch, because most batters are going to take it. Just to be safe, though, I try to put something on that grooved throw.

INTENTIONAL WALKS

I don't like intentional walks much more than I do unin-tentional ones, but as a pitcher I have very little to say about the decision. Sometimes, though, a manager will come out and say, "Do you want to pitch to this guy?"* and nine out of ten times I'd rather pitch to him than walk him, no matter who the batter is. The reason for this is something I mentioned earlier—the possibility of a big inning. I want to avoid a situation where, if I intentionally walk someone to put a man on first when first was open, or to load the bases, I take the chance of throwing a three-run or grand-slam homer. I've never thrown a grand slam in the big leagues, and hope I never do.

When you intentionally walk somebody, you create a situation where you *have* to pitch to the next batter—you can't pitch carefully and you can't pitch around him.

---

*Coming down the stretch in the 1973 National League pennant race Buzz Capra, pitching for the Mets, was asked whether he wanted to pitch to Willie Stargell or walk him and pitch to Richie Zisk of the Pirates. Capra chose to walk Stargell and pitch to Zisk, who was on a red-hot hitting streak. Zisk hit a good shot, but it was caught for an out.

Sometimes it works out well and saves the game, but too often all you do is present the other team with a chance for a big inning.

STRIKEOUTS

Control has a lot to do with strikeouts, although most of your good strikeout pitchers have overpowering fast balls or excellent breaking balls. Bert Blyleven, who strikes out 250 batters a year, has a great fast ball *and* a great curve ball; Nolan Ryan, although primarily a fast-ball pitcher, has both; Steve Carlton has a number of good pitches. Bob Gibson is overpowering with a good fast ball and a good slider.

In general, the good strikeout pitchers are primarily hard throwers with excellent stuff. Or they possess a good combination of pitches or an overpowering fast ball.

To throw strikeouts, first of all you've got to learn the strike zone.* The more you throw to batters, the better your feel for the strike zone will become. In addition, concentration and a lot of hard work on the sidelines will help you learn which pitches you're throwing are strikes and which aren't.

Throwing against a wall can be good practice. Pick out an area on the wall—maybe draw a rectangle—and

---

*This varies between the National and American leagues because the umpires position themselves differently. In the American, it's roughly from above the knees to the letters; in the National, from about the waist to the knees. As a high-ball pitcher, I have a little more trouble pitching with a National League umpire behind the plate, but with proper concentration I'm able to adjust.

keep pitching at it. Not only does this encourage you to concentrate and throw to that particular spot, it also makes you follow through.

THE SIGNIFICANCE OF STRIKEOUTS

My best strikeout total for a single game is 13. In my best season I struck out 199, and did I ever try to strike out that two-hundredth man! It was the seventh or eighth inning of a 1–1 ball game, and I knew, since the manager wanted us rested for the playoffs, I wouldn't be pitching any more after that inning. With two men out I faced Eddie Brinkman, and I tried everything on him; I even sidearmed him. The best I could do was get two strikes on him, and he finally popped up. Some people say 199 sounds more like a real strikeout total than an even 200, but I don't agree.

Strikeouts can give a pitcher a great deal of satisfaction. In the first game I pitched at the start of the 1969 season, after two years of arm trouble, I beat the Senators, 2–0, and struck out Frank Howard four times in a row. Those strikeouts helped signify that I was back to stay in the big leagues.

But big strikeout totals aren't always as important as people make them out to be.

The fact that you strike out a lot of men does not necessarily mean that you're pitching a good game. One thing that's sure: when you strike out a lot of batters, you're throwing a lot of pitches, and you're bound to tire. When a hitter swings at the first pitch and pops up, that's only one pitch you've thrown. But if you strike him out, he probably ran the count to 1–2 or 2–2, so you've thrown at least three pitches or more to strike him out. I've pitched games in which I've struck out a lot of batters, only to tire and have a man suddenly hit a three-run homer off me. Or I'll have a lot of good stuff to strike men out but I'll also be wild and give up a lot of walks.

I can remember a game I pitched against Minnesota. I threw 169 pitches, struck out twelve batters and had a 5–1 lead going into the ninth inning. They got two men on, and Eric Soderman, probably someone you never heard of, came to the plate. He fouled off six straight fast balls—I didn't want to walk him—and then smacked a home run to make it 5–4. The next man up got a bad-hop single. Then, with the count 2–2 on the next batter, I threw a curve ball right down the middle, but the umpire called it a ball. The next pitch was blooped for a single. There were more hits after that, and I didn't win the game.

Most times when I strike out a lot of batters, though, I've pitched a very good ball game. But believe me, I'd rather strike out only four or five men and not walk anybody than strike out a dozen and walk a lot of men. For instance, in the one no-hitter of my major league career, I struck out ten men but issued eight walks. It was no artistic success. A walk is not as bad as a base hit, because it can't be for an extra base. But it's exactly what it's called—a free pass—and usually you've put a man on there for nothing.

The truth is, strikeouts are important only in certain situations. Otherwise, they are just something glamorous and not especially significant. They're nice to have, and it's nice to know you can strike out someone when you want to. But a strikeout causes more pitches to be thrown than normally, and this puts more strain on your arm, something you can well do without.

Usually, then, I don't try for strikeouts very much, except for situations where if I don't get the strikeout I know I'm pretty surely going to give up an important run or let a runner get into scoring position when my team can't afford it. Specifically, I try for a strikeout in these situations:

1. A man on third base with less than two outs.

2. When there are runners on first and second and nobody out, and the hitter is trying to hit away. I'd like the chance at a double play, but I'd rather have a strikeout, on which the runners could not advance, than a grounder on which we manage to get just one out, with the lead runner able to advance to third base.

3. When there is a runner on second and none out, and we know they're trying to advance him to third, from where he could score on a sacrifice fly.

4. With the bases loaded and less than two outs.

5. Any other situation where we can't afford to have the runner advance—for instance, when the lead-off man is on base with no outs.

THE RISKS OF TRYING FOR A STRIKEOUT

Trying to strike a batter out isn't without its risks.

Often, for example, you'll have a tendency to overthrow, so you end up getting behind the batter, which results in a big inning, one that's probably bigger than the one you were trying to prevent.

For example, let's say the lead-off man doubles. To prevent him from being advanced to third and eventually scoring, you toil to pitch perfectly to the next batter. You pitch so carefully that you end up walking him, and now there are runners on first and second. Your troubles aren't over. The next man sacrifices them along, and the hitter after that drives in two runs with a base hit. They're on their way to a big inning.

You would have been better off to have conceded that lead runner and just made sure you didn't give them a big inning. (The key to successful pitching is probably not giving up more than one run an inning, although if you give up a run *every* inning, you're in trouble.)

Another hazard is that if you're the victim of a big inning early in the game, you may try to strike out a lot of men and get so tired from the attempt that you won't be able to go the full nine innings.

WASTED PITCHES: NO SUCH THING

When some pitchers get ahead of the count, they tend to think in terms of wasting a pitch. I don't believe in that idea. As I've probably said before, I think *every* pitch should have a purpose. You never really waste one. Say I've got an 0–2 count on a hitter. If I throw a pitch up and in, it's not really a wasted pitch, even though I know I'm going to throw it for a ball. The thing I'm trying to do is back the hitter off the plate and make him aware that it has an inside part.

If I decide to throw the pitch low and away, it's not my intention merely to throw it for a ball. I want to make it very close to the strike zone, with the idea of getting the batter to look for the ball away. The reason I want him to think this way is that I'm planning to throw my pitch up and in.

What I'm saying is that there should always be a reason to do something. You don't just want to throw a ball that's six or eight inches outside, or a pitch that's so far from the strike zone that the hitter knows immediately it's out of the zone. If I'm 0–2 on a batter, ultimately I want to get him out with a pitch on the outside corner. I'll throw him one in that area and not mind missing by a couple of inches, because he may fish for it—or at the very least, be set up for a later pitch.

Similarly, I might want to throw him a slider just to show him a slider, or a change-up for the sake of showing him a change, so that he might look for that pitch later on. Maybe I'll throw him a curve ball for a ball, which he might just chase after, even if it happens to be in the dirt.

In essence, you might consider what I throw on 0–2 a wasted pitch, but in my mind I'm not wasting it at all.

THE GOOD GAME

It might be a good idea to take a break here and talk about what the most important indicators of a well-pitched game are (besides winning the game). If I were asked to put them in order of importance to me, I'd say few earned runs, then few walks, followed by few hits, and finally, many strikeouts.

LOW ERA

How many runs you give up in a single game is not always a fair test of how well you pitched that day. Perhaps you pitched well and your teammates made costly errors. Or after they made errors, you pitched poorly and the other team scored five runs, but since they were unearned, they were not charged to your earned run average (ERA). Or you give up five earned runs one game and pitch a shutout the next. (Many minor-league pitchers have that lack of consistency and still manage to have something like a 2.75 earned run average.)

Nevertheless, for the most part your ERA is a true indicator of how well you pitch and how consistently you pitch. I pride myself on the fact that I've always had a low earned run average. I've been among the top three American League pitchers in that category most years I've been in the big leagues, and it was a big factor in my being voted the Cy Young Award in my league in 1973.

When you manage to keep your ERA down, it means you're doing well in two other priority categories, discussions of which follow.

FEW WALKS

To put it simply, when you walk a man nobody can help you get him out before he reaches first, whereas if you let him hit the ball, there's a chance the batted balls can be converted to outs. I try very hard not to walk anybody and thereby give the opposition free passage where nobody can help you.

The Oakland A's managed just *one* hit off our pitching when they beat us for the American League pennant in the final 1974 playoff game, 2–1. But our pitchers had given up *eleven* big walks, four of which accounted for the A's first run and winning margin.

FEW HITS

Through the 1973 season, I've had one major-league no-hitter and several near misses, including three one-hitters.

In the third game of the 1974 playoffs, I held Oakland to just four hits and one run (a homer on a 3–2 count by Sal Bando) but the A's Vida Blue did even better. He allowed us just two hits and no runs, and the A's won the game, 1–0. I didn't want to walk Bando, but after he homered, I wished I had. I was pleased with the way I pitched in that game and was frustrated about not winning. But there was nothing to say or do. I pitched well but Blue pitched a shutout. I didn't.

No-hitters are memorable but, believe it or not, they don't have the emotional buildup of a Series game or pennant clincher, because you don't go into the game thinking no-hitter.

About the fifth inning, I suppose, you do start thinking about it. But major-league pitchers often find themselves with no-hitters for four or five innings, and their prime consideration, if they're in a low-run contest, is just to conserve their energy so they can stick around and win the ball game.

On the other hand, if you've got something like an 8–0 lead, you don't really have to worry about being tired. So after the fifth inning, you say to yourself, "I'm going to concentrate on getting every hitter out," and go all out from that point on. Most of the games I've been involved in in which there was a real chance of a no-hitter have been contests in which we held a big lead.

The no-hitter I pitched in 1969 was an 8–0 game against the A's. It was my second game back after a back injury, and I walked eight men. So it was not, as I indicated earlier, an artistic triumph. In the ninth inning I walked one man after another until I reached someone I could retire. After walking Reggie Jackson, I had Dick Green on a 3–2 count and walked him on a close pitch, and then I walked Tommy Reynolds, an outfielder, because he was new and I didn't know how to pitch to him. Finally, I got to the fourth hitter, Larry Haney, who had played with the Orioles awhile, and he grounded out to shortstop.

I wouldn't have had that much suspense, except that earlier in the inning Danny Cater had hit a perfect double-play ball, which one of our infielders dropped; we managed to get only a force-out.

Your teammates talk to you, all right, during a no-hit bid. They kid around. Mike Cuellar and Dave McNally had both been through it with one-hitters. During my no-hitter, Cuellar walked up to me and gave me the choke sign when I went out there—and I did, I choked. But I was able to give it back to him and manage the no-hitter.

In 1973 I came very close to another one. This one was a perfect game for eight and a third innings, and I think I would have had the no-hitter except that I was trying for the perfect game.

With one out in the ninth inning, I went to a 2–0 count on Ken Suarez of Texas. I didn't want to spoil the perfect game by walking him. So instead of throwing him a slider as I normally would have—even in a no-hit bid—and taken a chance on walking him, I threw him a fast ball. That was fatal. Because of the 2–0 count, our shortstop, Mark Belanger, moved a little to his right into the hole, and Suarez hit my fast ball exactly where Belanger had been—for a base hit. But that's one of those things.

It's funny. I had an upset stomach that day and almost missed my start. Then, when the Orioles scored five runs in the very first inning, a rare treat for the pitcher, who happened to be me, Earl Weaver turned to me and said, "Imagine how much sicker you'd be if you were home in bed and we'd scored those five runs." I answered, "You're right."

Another time, I had a no-hitter going through seven innings against Cleveland. In the eighth inning I faced George Hendrick, a breaking-ball hitter who had hit about twenty of his twenty-five home runs on breaking balls. I threw him a low slider and he socked a line drive base hit right through my legs.

Otherwise, it was a pretty good game.

THE IMPORTANCE OF ROTATION

At whatever playing level you are, it's important that you pitch regularly, in the same rotation. It's the best way to get into a consistent groove.

The Mets pitch on a five-day rotation, the Orioles on a four-day system, which I prefer—although when you play forty straight games in the middle of summer, it's nice to get an occasional day off to sort of "regroup."

But whatever the interval between your starts, it's helpful to work on a regular schedule—and frequently. The more you do something, the more consistently and better you'll be able to perform. Your windup will have a better rhythm to it, and other aspects of your pitching are bound to improve.

Pitching only every six or seven days is going to make it more difficult for you, although there will be times when you're fatigued and you'll appreciate an extra day between starts. But it's nice to be able to pitch in regular rotation so you can get maximum benefit from your between-starts schedule, and then set yourself to give your best performance on a particular day.

Conditioning

MAJOR-LEAGUERS practice every day, and so should you.

PITCHING

The best practice for a pitcher, obviously, is pitching. Pitch to a catcher, if possible from a mound of the same height you'll use in a game, and with the distance between the mound and the plate that is regulation in your league. If you pitch from a flat surface, rather than a mound, your windup will tend to change a little bit.

If you don't have a catcher to practice throwing to, then pitch at a target, say a marked-off strike zone on a brick wall. You can also set up strings to form the outline of the strike zone, and aim for that.

When you're playing catch, throw the ball with a purpose. For instance, throw it to the level of the shoulders of the person you're catching with, or aim for the middle of his chest. Often we'll play a game, especially during those required twenty-minute catches we have in spring training (see page 140), where you get one point for hitting the fellow from the waist up and two points if you ·hit him in the face. We don't mean literally "hit" him—he's catching the ball—but being on target. If the ball is thrown outside the other fellow's body, you get no points. This sort of game disciplines your concentration when you throw the ball. You can make up your own game for the same purpose.

In addition to throwing on the sidelines in spring training and before games, the pitcher in that day's lineup has the chance to throw to his catcher before the start of each inning. In the majors, eight warm-up pitches are permissible before each. You should use the warm-ups to meet whatever pitching needs you have that particular game. For instance, sometimes I use them just to loosen up. But other times, when I've been guilty of my biggest lapse in concentration and have been getting my pitches up too much, I use the warm-ups to concentrate on getting my pitches down a little bit.

It's important that when somebody warms you up, he takes a normal catching position, because if he stands up, you'll tend to throw the ball higher than you would normally.

It's a great advantage if, when you're practice pitching, you have someone stand in at the plate in the role of the batter, because otherwise you'll find it a lot different from pitching in the actual game. When I warm up before a game, I always have somebody stand there so, among other things, I can see how my breaking ball is breaking in respect to the hitter. This can also help you overcome the tendency to throw off the batter instead of to your catcher.

Can there ever be too *much* practice? Not really, although you can throw so much that your arm becomes tired. When it gets very tired, stop throwing. Not that you're likely to injure your arm, but it won't have its normal liveliness, and you might as well stop than just go through the motions with your concentration waning.

SHAGGING FLIES AND PEPPER

Every day of the season I shag flies, and I really enjoy it. Not only is it kind of a pleasant challenge for a pitcher to go chasing after fly balls in batting practice, but it also allows me to do two things: get in some extra running, and work on my hand-eye coordination, both of which are so important to a pitcher.

Hand in hand with shagging flies, another valuable pastime is playing pepper—in which several players alternately throw to a batter and field the balls he hits at close range.

The American League pitchers don't hit any more during the regular season, now that the designated hitting rule is in effect, but pepper does help your hitting—and who knows? In an interleague game it can come in handy. For instance, Ken Holtzman, the A's pitcher, got a key hit in the 1973 World Series against the Mets and continued his Series hitting spree in 1974 against the Dodgers. (One of my most memorable games in the big leagues was my first one, when I hit a home run to right field off Jim Bouton, the famous author who was then a pitcher. Having grown up in New York, I found it a great

137

thrill to beat the Yankees.) Aside from helping your hitting, pepper helps your hands and general coordination. The pepper we play on the Orioles is a pretty quick game, and the hitter does rap the ball pretty hard, so your overall reflexes are sharpened.

TAKING CARE OF YOURSELF

A pitcher has to be in better condition than any other player on the team. It's true he doesn't have the day-to-day grind of the team's regular third baseman or short-stop, but he's got to have his respiratory system in excellent shape, and his legs have to be stronger than those of the others. He's got to prepare himself mentally and physically to pitch every fourth or fifth day, and nervous anticipation before a start can rob him of sleep and proper diet.

More than anything, a pitcher needs stamina because his is the most grueling job of anyone's. If you're not in the best shape, it will show in your pitching. If your legs aren't in condition, you're going to get tired. If your arm's not in shape, it's going to get tired. If you don't eat the proper food, you're not going to have the proper energy to pitch.

If you're like most young players, you probably don't appreciate the God-given ability you have. Possibly because you don't know any better, you don't take proper care of your arm and you use it almost as a toy, throwing when and how the mood strikes you.

Playing professional ball is a great learning experience. You mature tremendously. It's unbelievable how much

I've changed and developed—for the better—since I was eighteen years old, in terms of the things I've learned about taking care of myself. Let me share some of these with you.

CONDITIONING YOUR ARM

The most important thing to remember is you have only one pitching arm. If you injure it, it might never recover, and your pitching days are over.

Having had arm troubles, I'm very appreciative of the fact that my arm has responded to treatment. Part of that good fortune is due to the fact that I never abused my arm. Some young pitchers do abuse theirs; they don't realize that it's just like any other muscle in their body, and that it has to be prepared and warmed up properly. You can't just go out and use it to start throwing a baseball as hard as you can, any more than you would go out and suddenly start running full speed without having first stretched your legs or jogged or otherwise built up to it.

That's why, when you warm up, you have to start throwing the ball in a rather slow manner until your arm is stretched out. Until you warm up, the muscle is cold and susceptible to injury. That's why the pitcher is allowed the luxury of throwing practice pitches at the start of each inning, and a starting pitcher has ten or fifteen minutes to warm up.

As you become more experienced, you may find that it takes less—or more—time to get loose. That varies from pitcher to pitcher. Some need only about five pitches to be ready. When I first came to the big leagues, eight pitches were all I needed for my arm to be completely loose, but now I take better care of it and I warm up more gradually, to make sure I don't tear anything that isn't normally torn in pitching.*

We used to have a lot of arm trouble on the Orioles because we used to just start throwing on the sidelines without first building up our arms. Then we started a spring training routine that we still follow. For twenty minutes every day of spring training we play catch. We start about sixty or seventy feet from one another and then spread out to ninety or one hundred feet. We don't wind up, but we do throw each ball from our normal throwing position. As an overhand pitcher, I will throw overhand, and so on. Twenty minutes of this every day—besides throwing on the mound—is bound to strengthen your arm. It's not so much that this sort of "play" enables you to throw harder, but it builds your arm up without hurting it.

Immediately after I've pitched a game, I put my elbow into ice, because the more bleeding you get in your arm from the torn muscle fiber and little blood vessels, the longer it takes you to recuperate. Putting the elbow on ice restricts the bleeding, and I don't have anywhere near as much blood flow through my arm until the following day.

---

*It's normal that when you pitch, muscle fibers are torn. When you come to spring training, scar tissue adhesions have formed where muscles have been torn in pitching. What you have to do is stretch those muscles out and break those adhesions. Even between starts, when the torn muscle fibers start to heal, you're going to have to stretch out some muscle fiber and get blood back in that area. This is why your arm feels extremely stiff when you first throw. The most important thing to do between starts is throw with your natural delivery. Don't throw any differently than you do in an actual ball game.

Two days after I've pitched, I throw to a catcher over a regulation distance from a mound on the sidelines for between ten and twenty minutes. This is my opportunity to work on my different pitches. The next day I usually play catch a little bit with one of the other pitchers or one of the infielders. I'm careful not to overextend my arm; I just want to keep my muscles stretched out.

In the off-season, to keep adhesions from forming, I do some exercise with a five-pound weight over my head and out to the right a little. Beware, though, of using weights without proper instruction. You might check into isometric exercises, but there, too, use caution.

KEEPING YOUR ARM WARM

It's very important to keep your arm warm, because if it cool off, its muscles, like any others, have a tendency to tighten up. You should keep it warm at all times, day or night, sleeping or awake, walking outdoors or traveling in a car. If your arm gets warm and then cools off, the blood flow is not as good and it's easy to pull the muscle.

So keep your arm warm at all times. Always wear a jacket when you're not pitching, even if it's a warm night. And you should wear a sweatshirt to absorb your perspiration before it evaporates and chills you. The first year I was in the majors I hurt myself because the sweatshirt I wore was so thin. I didn't realize how much I had been perspiring, and that my back had cooled off, and I went out and threw a pitch and pulled a muscle in my back. I was out a month.

The injury bothered me all winter, and I went down to Clearwater, Florida, to the instructional league. The coach there asked me whether I wore a heavy sweatshirt.

I told him I didn't, and he advised me that I should. I followed his advice and I've never had problems like that since.

KEEPING YOUR HANDS WARM

Early or late in the season, when the weather is cool and crisp, your hands can become slick, and when they do, you don't have the feel in them that you normally would. A lot of pitchers go to their mouths because saliva gives their skin some feeling and takes away the slickness in their fingertips. The easiest way to warm your pitching hand is put it in your pocket, or to blow into your hand.

LEGS: MORE IMPORTANT THAN YOU THINK

People who don't know any better think the pitching arm is all that matters for a pitcher. Legs are equally important, because if you don't have the momentum you need going to home plate, you can't possibly expect to drive correctly. You have to develop your legs, which is why the importance of running can't be stressed enough.

A pitcher like myself throws between 120 and 140 pitches a game, plus another 120 warming up and 72 more if he manages to go nine innings (eight pitches before each inning). Count them up and you're somewhere in the neighborhood of 330 pitches. As you pitch, you're constantly thrusting forward, with your legs supplying the drive. I don't drive as hard as a man like Tom Seaver does, but still I know how much I rely on my legs. I always feel that if I can get my legs in shape, there's no reason I should get tired.

You'll find that all your good pitchers, players like Warren Spahn, who lasted a very long time in baseball, have always kept themselves and their legs in excellent shape. On the other side of the coin, it was his bad legs that ended Mickey Mantle's career prematurely.

I try to run a mile or a mile and a half every night of the off-season. During the season, my routine consists of running a lot between starts. On the first day after I pitch, I'll probably run about twenty sprints from one foul line to the other, which totals roughly a mile and a half or two miles, and I'll run the sprints at a pretty rapid pace. Our ball club does the sprints collectively, so the total distance and time are pretty much controlled. On the second day I'll run eighteen or twenty foul-line sprints. On the third day I cut down my running to about twelve laps. And then the fourth day I pitch.

In addition to running, I do other things to keep my legs in shape. Every day I have my hamstring muscles stretched by the trainer, because the hamstrings and the lower back are areas that pitchers sometimes hurt because of all the pressure there. You have to be limber in those parts of the body. At one time I had some back problems, and found they were due to the fact that my hamstrings weren't as limber or stretched out as they should be. So I just lie on the table and have my trainer lock my legs and lift them as high over my head as he can.

Chances are you don't have a trainer waiting to serve you, but you can still accomplish the desired effect by yourself. Sit on the ground in a sort of hurdler's stance, with one leg out in front of you and one leg out to the side. Bend your upper torso and try to touch the ground. This will stretch one hamstring. Then reverse the position of your legs and stretch the other hamstring.

The groin area is also very important, because there's so much stress there in pitching. To strengthen and stretch that area, I spread my legs and shift my weight from one side to the other.

Other areas to keep in shape are the rib cage and lower back. Tear a rib muscle and it will be three weeks before you're back in action. To strengthen the rib-cage and lower-back muscles, I do a lot of toe-touching exercises without bending my knees, and I turn or twist from one side to another with my arms outstretched.

You have to do these preventive-type exercises regularly.

I do two other exercises to strengthen my back muscles. In one I lie on my back with my legs straight over my head and my knees tucked to my chest. Then I rock up and down to stretch my lower-back muscles. In the other I lie on my back, with my legs straight up, and try to touch the ground behind my head.

OFF-SEASON ATHLETICS

You don't want your body to hibernate in the winter. Play some kind of ball, ride a bike, do calisthenics, to keep yourself limber and your muscles toned.

But during the baseball season or in the off-season, it's best to avoid activities like bowling, which puts a different type of stress on your arm than what you're accustomed to in pitching.

It's amazing how just using a hammer, for instance,

can affect your muscles. They're trained to do one thing, and if suddenly they're called upon to do something different, they may get sore. If they're muscles that are an integral part of pitching, to use them in another, strenuous activity will have an adverse effect on your pitching performance.

DIET AND REST

OVERWEIGHT

Being overweight can be a big problem for a ball player, especially at the start of the season, so don't overeat, and exercise to keep your weight in check. I compare being overweight to running around with a five-pound weight on each leg. It makes running that much harder.

Excellent athletes like Frank Robinson, Willie Mays, and Hank Aaron always kept themselves in good shape, their weight included. Except compared to when he first broke in, Aaron, for instance, hasn't changed much in weight at all.

My own ideal playing weight is about 195. I used to weigh 210, but after playing in Puerto Rico, it just went down and it's stayed there. During the off-season, I lose weight because I don't eat as much. In season I make sure I eat enough to have sufficient energy to play my best.

FOOD AND DRINK

I never eat anything during a game. But just before one, if I'm hungry, I may have an orange or pear, if I can get hold of it. Like anything with sugar in it, fruit is a good source of energy. It's better than candy, which isn't good for your teeth, but I must admit I'll sometimes have a candy bar for quick energy before a game if that's all that's available in the clubhouse.

The day of a game in which you're going to pitch, make sure you eat a balanced meal and give yourself enough time to digest your food. Both on the day I pitch and the day before, I try to include a lot of protein in my diet, so I drink a lot of milk and eat a lot of eggs.

In general I eat good basic foods, with only an occasional piece of candy. Besides milk and eggs, I try to eat a substantial amount of beef and vegetables. The old saying that "you are what you eat" is especially true when applied to athletes, so watch your diet. As a firm believer in proper conditioning, I don't smoke or drink alcoholic beverages.

I've found that, contrary to what a lot of people believe, drinking water during a game in hot weather isn't bad for you—providing you don't drink excessive amounts. I'll pitch three or four innings in the heat, and feel I have to drink fluids continually to keep from getting dehydrated. I also find it keeps me fresh.

TABLETS AND PILLS

Also to keep from getting dehydrated, I take salt tablets, and they may be a factor in preventing cramps.

But as far as pep pills and things of that sort are concerned, I've never tried them, although others have. There are a number of reasons for my attitude. First, I don't need any sort of stimulant to boost my enthusiasm for the game because I enjoy what I'm doing so much. Also, when I'm on the mound I want to have complete control of my faculties. I want to know what I'm doing and why I'm doing it.

Pills have given a lot of athletes a false sense of security, making them feel so good that they try to do things they aren't really able to. This goes against the principle of pitching within your capabilities and trying to realize those capabilities to the fullest potential. If you try things you're not capable of doing, you're not likely to succeed.

REST

Closely connected with your overall physical condition and how well you perform, of course, is rest.

The day before I pitch, I like to sleep as long as I can. I try not to let my sleep be interrupted by calls or anything else. You should get at least eight to ten hours of sleep the night before you pitch, because not only does it contribute to your physical well-being, it also helps the mental aspect of your game. When you're well rested, it just seems that you can concentrate better.

Right after I've pitched, I usually have trouble sleeping because I'm all keyed up. The next night, though, I'm so tired from not having slept the previous night that I get a pretty good sleep; I can just about fall asleep anywhere I happen to be. Two nights before I pitch, I find I've got to get a good night's sleep or fatigue is going to catch up with me on the mound.

Sometimes when I've pitched Saturday afternoon and then have to pitch Tuesday night (which means only two and a half days' rest between starts), I'll really feel tired in my legs. And the day after pitching a night game I'll feel it there, too.

There are times when the pitching arm tightens up a little and doesn't have its usual flexibility and strength. And occasionally during the summer, my legs may get tired and not have their usual bounce. But normally this doesn't happen because I try to condition them as well as I can.

If your legs are feeling tired, you can taper off your running a little, while keeping up your conditioning exercises. For example, we do twenty laps a day in spring training, then eighteen when we come north until August, when we cut to about fourteen laps. By then we're pretty well conditioned.

BUILDING ENDURANCE

Often when pitchers who are used to being starters are assigned to the bullpen for relief duty, they find it difficult to pitch many innings because they just haven't been pitching enough. This illustrates that the best way for a pitcher to build endurance is pitch. Your legs and arms have to be in good shape, and you have to use them regularly by pitching.

INJURY, ACCIDENT, ILLNESS

Rest and diet will cut down on your chances of illness, and your overall conditioning should either help make you less susceptible to injury or reduce the severity, or at least help you bounce back from injury. I hurt my back and was out of competition for forty-two days, but I was able to run and keep my legs in shape and make a comeback.

If injury is inevitable, you're a lot better off if it happens late in the season when your arm is built up and strong than early in the season, when you're not yet at the top of your form. Early in the season an injury to one part of your body is likely to have a bad effect on another part of your body. Let's say that early in April, after you've finished spring training, you hurt your leg. Your arm is going to be adversely affected by the layoff. But suffer that same leg injury in mid-season, when your arm is fairly strong, and you'll be able to make a relatively easy comeback after a layoff of two or three weeks.

Of course, you can't very well schedule your injuries. And it's difficult to avoid injuries entirely; they develop from so many different causes.

I had an arm injury that came from pitching too many innings at too early an age, combined with doing some painting on my new house, which put added strain on my arm. The overall pressure of the pitching, the immaturity of my body, and my extracurricular housework combined to make one tendon in my arm sore. I couldn't get a good diagnosis of which tendon was affected, so I started favoring my arm altogether.

The worst offshoot of an arm injury is that you usually start throwing differently. And when you do that, you usually end up injuring another part of your arm. Obviously, it's important when your arm pains you to go to a good doctor and get the proper type of care.

DON'T PLAY WITH AN INJURY

Some players, to be heroic or because they're worried about their jobs, continue to play with injuries when they really shouldn't. I think when your body hurts, it's usually trying to tell you that something is wrong. I'm not suggesting that you hang up your glove the moment you feel an ache; there's a fine line between an arm being stiff and sore and being injured. Experience will help you differentiate. I know that pains I feel now at age twenty-nine are different from pains I felt when I was twenty-one. I used to live in constant fear that if my arm hurt me, I surely had an injury; now I know that an aching arm is part of my profession.

But having said this, I still believe you shouldn't continue to play when it means risking permanent injury. That's true of professional ball players, who have more reason to swallow their pain and hang in there. It's certainly true of amateur ball players. Get what's hurting you checked out. Playing with something that could be serious certainly doesn't help you, and it doesn't do your team much good, either. Often you have to play when your muscles aren't feeling 100 percent. But when something is bothering you—mentally or physically— you can't do your job the way you should.

THE PHYSICAL AFFECTS THE MENTAL

The day I first signed with the Orioles I was a passenger in a car going 70 miles an hour whose driver fell asleep. The accident demolished the car and injured my left knee so badly that it eventually required surgery to remove a blood clot and cyst. That spring I was supposed to report to the Orioles in Miami, but instead I had to go to minor-league spring training, and I missed a month. Because of the operation, my knee was so sore it didn't afford me the flexibility needed to pitch well. And worrying about my inability to bend my knees took something off my concentration in pitching. Try not to let your physical problems affect your pitching mentality.

SOME ACCIDENTS CAN BE AVOIDED

Jim Lonborg asked me to go skiing with him the year he hurt his knee in a skiing accident. He was a novice skier, and at the time of his accident was outfitted with faulty equipment, I think. I declined the invitation because I'd never skied, and it seemed foolish for me to risk injury doing something I hadn't done before. I do play basketball, tennis, and golf, but in basketball (we have an Orioles team) I make sure to avoid situations where I'm likely to be knocked to the floor. During the season, because I'm afraid of hurting my elbow or another part of my pitching arm, I play tennis left-handed. And as much as I love golf, I don't play it during the season because a different set of muscles is involved.

You can't be too careful if baseball is your profession, although there's always a chance of a freak accident— Tom Seaver, for instance, hurt his back moving a carton in his basement, an injury that could have cost the Mets the pennant in 1973, and Cecil Upshaw almost tore a finger off his pitching hand *pantomiming* going up for a dunk shot.

BLISTERS

One of the occupational hazards of pitching is the development of blisters. Because of the constant pressure of the seams of the ball on the skin, I've had calluses on my middle finger and on the side of the thumb. The buildup of tissue on the outside of your skin becomes hard, and you have to file down the accumulation to avoid internal pressure.

It's hard to escape developing blisters because of the constant friction. Once your hand toughens up, the problem isn't likely to be severe. The important thing is to keep them filed down before they become so hard that they cause bruises when pressure is exerted on them. Make sure, though, that what you file them with is sterilized, and that you don't go down so far that you cause bleeding and possible infection.

YOUR NAILS

It's important to keep your nails well manicured, so there aren't any sharp edges and so your nails won't bite into the skin or cause any cuts.

Nails can be helpful delivering a knuckle ball. Eddie Fisher, who used to pitch for us, always worried about tearing a fingernail because he threw a knuckle ball. But a torn nail can be annoying to any type of pitcher.

Strategy in
Pitching

S U C C E S S F U L   P I T C H I N G is as much a matter of head work as anything else. Being able to throw the ball high and hard isn't enough, nor, by itself, is control. You've got to be able to figure out how to pitch in particular situations and against particular hitters—and then be able to do it. Let's talk about some of the elements of pitching strategy, keeping in mind that no stratagem is going to work every time.

STUDYING THE HITTERS

Studying hitters is fundamental to any successful pitching strategy. You do it not only when you face them, but before and after.

The best way to study hitters is to categorize them as to whether they're high-ball or low-ball hitters, whether they like the ball away or in, and whether they are breaking-ball or fast-ball hitters. When you determine these facts, you have to examine your own style and ability, and then make your decision about what you're going to try to do with a particular hitter.

Of course, the circumstances and the situation will dictate what you're going to do. If the man can't hit a breaking ball, that's what you want to throw. But if you can't get your curve over that day, you're going to have to figure out another way to get him out. The same thing applies if he can't hit the fast ball but you don't have one.

You should watch hitters carefully to see such things as whether they wait very well on the breaking ball or whether they're out on their front foot, whether they're first-ball fast-ball hitters, and so forth.

WATCHING OTHER PITCHERS

One way to learn about opposing hitters, especially if they're from a different league, is to watch how they do against other pitchers on your team. This doesn't always work. When we go to the playoffs, for example, and Mike Cuellar and Dave McNally have pitched the first two games for us, it's hard for me to visualize myself pitching like they do, since I'm not left-handed, I'm not a breaking-ball pitcher, and I don't throw screwballs. So what I try to do is watch somebody with a style similar to mine in action against that ball club.

KEEPING A CHART

You'll hear people talk about the "book" on a particular hitter. That doesn't mean there's actually a book to read

—although some pitchers keep one—it's more a matter of common knowledge, information about a hitter that veterans pass on to newcomers, or what someone who has just come over from another team or the other league passes on to you. Most of the time, though, you have to find out for yourself, through the experience of facing the hitter several times.

Even though there's usually no actual book, teams keep pitch-by-pitch charts of games that tell what pitches what batters hit, what the count was when they hit them, where the pitches were, and to what field the balls were hit.

On our club and most others, the chart of a particular game is kept by the man who is due to be the starting pitcher for the next day. It gives him something constructive to do, and it makes him keenly aware of who's hitting what, which could be especially helpful to him because it will be fresh in his mind the next day when he faces that team (unless it was the last day of the series).

On many major-league teams, the player who's charting the game sits behind home plate, where you can get the best picture of where the pitches are—not only whether they're up or down, but also whether they're in or out. We sit in the dugout when we chart, which doesn't afford as good a view.

The type and location of the pitch, whether it's a ball or a strike, whether the man hits it and, if so, where, are all simply noted by dots and other symbols on the chart. "F-9," for example, means the man flied out to right field. We'd put "3-Belt" to indicate that he hit a slider at the belt, and an arrow to describe where the ball traveled.

SCOUTING REPORTS

Scouting reports are helpful, especially around World Series time and for the All-Star Game, when you're going to be dealing with hitters you don't play against regularly.

Most hitters prefer pitches in the middle of the plate, belt high. But I can remember 1970, when I was going to pitch the first game of the World Series against the Cincinnati Reds, and we went down the Reds' lineup in a long meeting.

Joe Morgan, they said, was a high fast-ball hitter; Bobby Tolan, high fast-ball hitter; Johnny Bench, high fast-ball hitter; Tony Perez, high fast-ball hitter, and so on down the line. Finally, I said, "Wait a minute. I'm a high fast-ball pitcher, and if these guys are all high fast-ball hitters, why am I pitching the first game?" But that didn't change things. Of that imposing lineup, it was Lee May who really crushed us that Series.

Scouting reports have their limitations. Often, for instance, they'll describe a man as a high fast-ball hitter, but not say whether or not he's a *good* fast-ball hitter. Or they may not mention that he's not a good high fast-ball hitter when the pitcher is ahead of the count and after he's gotten two breaking balls over. So you have to examine and analyze the contents of a scouting report. And you've also got to ask yourself, "Can I do what the scouting report suggests?"

Most of the time when I see a scouting report, I get scared to death. I wonder how I can possibly do it. But most of the reports advise something as simple as "pitch him high and tight" or "low and away." For that kind of advice, you don't need a scouting report, because the percentages are going to be with you, if you can do it.

CLUBHOUSE MEETINGS

Before we play each team at the beginning of the season, we have a clubhouse meeting that lasts half an hour or forty-five minutes. We go over all the hitters, and decide on how the left-handed pitchers and right-handed pitchers will throw to each batter.

The game plan, if you want to call it that, usually revolves around how the pitcher is going to do—what he can do and how well he's going to pitch to the hitters' weaknesses.

DEALING WITH THE HITTERS

The "book" on hitters, game charts, scouting reports, clubhouse meetings, and your own observations will tell you about the opposing hitters' weaknesses, but knowing their weaknesses isn't enough. Unfortunately, you can't always do what you want to take advantage of those weaknesses.

Ideally, against the Oakland ball club, I want to throw Bert Campaneris low-and-away sliders all day long, because he's a fast-ball hitter. And against Joe Rudi, a tough out, I want to keep the ball down, my breaking balls low and away, and my fast balls either low and away or up and tight.

But a pitcher can't always do those things, so he has to ask himself: "What am I doing today? Am I getting my fast ball over? Do I have good control of my fast ball, or should I try to throw a breaking ball because I can't spot my fast ball?" You have to determine your answers as you warm up and as the game progresses.

MOVING THE BALL AROUND

Earlier we talked about the importance of moving a ball around on the hitter. That's a fundamental of pitching strategy. You don't want the batter to be able to predict where every pitch is coming and be able to get set for it. Therefore, you should mix up what you throw.

Obviously, hitters become better hitters when you keep pitching them one way and they can start looking for the ball in one place. If you've been getting them out by pitching to one particular area, their common sense will tell them they have to do something about it. Then you have to do something to counteract that.

If a hitter starts out standing over the plate, you move him back with an inside pitch, so that now when you go outside with a pitch, it looks farther outside to him because he's no longer up to the plate. You've got to keep him guessing.

GOOD HITTERS AND THEIR WEAKNESSES

Good hitters have their weaknesses, just as bad hitters do. One big difference, though, is that the good hitters' shortcomings aren't as apparent.

You can't consistently pitch to the same place on a good hitter and expect to get away with it. For example, you can get Dick Allen out by pitching him up and in or low and away. But if you keep pitching him one of these ways, he will look for the ball there and compensate. If he's looking for the ball up and in, he'll just move away a little bit, and it's no longer up and in. More likely, he'll hit it up and away.

With poor hitters, though, you can go to their weaknesses almost all the time and be pretty confident of getting them out.

Then again, a pitcher can't always do what he wants to do. If I knew I could go out and get the ball low and away all day, or high and in, it would make the game pretty easy for me.

FIRST-BALL HITTERS

There are many notorious first-ball hitters in the major leagues, some of whom will swing only if it's a particular type of pitch. Mickey Stanley is probably the best of the good first-ball fast-ball hitters. Gates Brown is a good one, and so is Bobby Murcer, who used to hit about .260 but now is in the neighborhood of .300 because he became more selective. Al Kaline used to guess a lot.

My feeling is that when you're facing a first-ball fast-ball hitter, you have to keep the pitch out of the middle of the plate. It's important to make it a good pitch, with a lot on it, because he knows a fast ball is coming and will probably swing at it. Throw him a breaking ball and he's probably going to lay off it, and if the pitch is not a strike, you're behind him.

That's why I'll inevitably throw a fast ball to a first-ball fast-ball hitter, because if it's a good pitch and he swings, he'll probably make out and I'll be on my way to an easy inning. It doesn't matter that he expects the fast ball, if I throw it well enough and to the right spot. I also know I'm going to get more fast balls over than I am curve balls.

WHEN YOU'RE BEHIND THE HITTER

When I've got a 2–0 count on a hitter, he's pretty sure to

be expecting a fast ball to be next. I find that's an ideal time to throw a slider. First of all, a slider moves just enough that the batter is likely to get out in front of it and hit it with the end of the bat. Also, a slider is easier to throw over the plate than a curve ball, so if you're going to throw a slider, the time to do it is when you're behind the batter.

DEALING WITH A MAN WHO UPSWINGS

Most good hitters have a level swing, or one in which they hit down on the ball to give it overspin. There are some exceptions. Superstrong hitters like Harmon Killebrew and Frank Howard sort of golf the ball, although Howard's swing is pretty level, while Killebrew's had a little arc in it. Basically, your good hitters swing a bat in a pretty level plane wherever the ball is.

When you're pitching against a batter who normally swings up, pitch him up, because a ball down will be in his favored area.

MAKING A BATTER HIT IN THE AIR

When you want a batter to hit the ball in the air, throw him a fast ball up in the strike zone, either on the outside or inside part of the plate. Or jam him so he can't get the bat around.

MAKING A BATTER HIT ON THE GROUND

To get a batter to hit the ball on the ground, keep the ball down. A good hard slider is an excellent double-play ball, because often the batter will try to get out there to pull what appears to be a fast ball and is fooled. He commits himself to swinging at a fast ball, with his weight already on the front foot, only to have the ball suddenly break away and down from him. The bat is already there and he can't hold back, and the result is a ground ball hit at the end of the bat to the shortstop.

If you have a good sharp curve ball, it can be effective against the batter who hits from the same side of the plate as you pitch from (a right-handed hitter if you're a right-handed pitcher).

DEALING WITH A BUNT SITUATION

When you're pitching in an apparent bunt situation, throw a high fast ball, preferably one that's in on the hitter. On a pitch thrown high, the hitter has to get his bat up, and then anything can happen—usually to your benefit—such as a pop-up. You don't want to pitch the ball down, because that would give the ball too much of a chance to hit the bottom of the bat, which would be good for the bunter.

A good slider isn't a bad pitch to try in this circumstance, and although most people advise against throwing a curve ball in a bunting situation, a good hard one can be very effective because of the element of surprise. Especially if you've been throwing high fast balls, if you suddenly throw a curve ball—if it's a good one—you'll have the bunter lunging at it. Avoid a *slow* curve ball, however, because the batter can follow the ball all the way down and then bunt it.

There are times would-be bunters will let the first pitch go by, figuring that it's going to be a high fast ball. In that case, you've got to be careful of what you do next. For instance, Oriole batters will often take the first pitch in the bunt situation, hoping it's out of the strike zone. If it is a ball, we figure the pitcher will still expect a bunt and

161

will come in with a fast ball. This time, we swing for a base hit.

So as a pitcher in this situation, beware. You can try the high-and-tight fast ball, which is awfully hard to hit, but whatever you throw, make sure it comes over the plate with something on it. You don't have to throw it as hard as you can, but you should make sure it has good stuff. You don't want to just lay it in there, in case the man is not bunting on your second pitch.

I can cite a sad experience in this connection. Our team, Santurce, was playing San Juan in the Puerto Rican Winter League for the championship. We were enjoying a 2–0 lead behind the pitching of Reuben Gomez, the former Giant hurler. San Juan had runners on first and second, and there were no outs. Gomez was sure that the next batter, Tony Taylor (who now plays for the Phillies), had the bunt sign, so he just laid the pitch in there, and Taylor hit a three-run homer to beat us in the playoff.

It was a matter of the pitcher overthinking and not throwing the ball as well as he should have. If he had thrown the ball as he otherwise might have, Taylor's home run might have been a catchable fly ball to left field instead.

You can't take things for granted.

PREVENTING THE HIT AND RUN

You don't always know the other team is going to try a hit-and-run play. When you do suspect it, what should you do?

Most batters trying to complete a hit-and-run play aim at hitting behind the runner, but still probably prefer the pitch inside so they can "inside-out" the ball. That's why I try to pitch outside.

Even though most right-handed batsmen hit a ball away from them to right field, they still want to make sure that, in swinging, their hands go through before the bat and that the bat is in position to push the ball to right. They like to be able to "throw" their hands at the ball, so they prefer a pitch inside. Dick Groat, a master hit-and-run practitioner, liked the ball in much better than a ball away.

Pitching batters like this away isn't enough, though; you've got to try to keep the ball down as well. Avoid a breaking ball in this situation, because the hitter is prepared to wait long to make sure he doesn't jump out and pull the ball. When I suspect a hit-and-run play is in the making, I usually throw something hard—a fast ball or slider.

DEALING WITH THE CONTACT HITTER

I think of a contact or "Ping-Pong" type of hitter as someone you have to try to make hit the ball over your outfielder's head.

Against a man like Campy Campaneris of the A's, a pretty good fast-ball hitter, you move in your outfield and infield. You make him try to hit the ball past your infielders to get his hits, rather than concede him any that he can beat out purely on speed. In the outfield, you don't want to give him any base hits in front of you. Instead, you want to make him try to hit the ball over the outfielder's head; the percentage being that he isn't going to be able to. The same applies to players like Del Unser,

Eddie Brinkman, or Horace Clark.

The third and first basemen play off the line for percentage reasons, too; most balls are hit in the hole between shortstop and third base, or the hole between first and second. It's only late in the game, when a double could lead to a game-tying or game-winning run, that they guard the foul lines. It's the same idea dealing with "Ping-Pong" hitters. Play the percentages and keep the ball down.

DEALING WITH THE POWER HITTER

Almost always, power hitters are high-ball hitters, so I try to keep the ball down in the strike zone against them. I also try to pitch them away, because I know they're strong enough to hit the ball out of the park down the line, so I want them to have to hit it to the opposite field. They have to be super-strong to hit the ball out of the park that way—the opposite field—and I'd much rather give up a double to right center than a home run to left center.

There are times, though, when you're going to pitch power against power. This depends on the count, the game situation, and how much stuff you have. For instance, I remember being able to get Harmon Killebrew out well by pitching him up and in. He liked the pitch there and saw it very well, but he just couldn't catch up with the ball.

I knew if I pitched him over the plate, where he could get his arms extended, it wouldn't have mattered whether the ball was outside, inside, or right in the middle of the plate; he'd still get the ball out to right center. In one of the best games I ever pitched in the big leagues, I had a one-run lead. Then I threw a low-and-away fast ball, and Killebrew walloped it out over the right field bullpen. But that's an exception, thank heaven.

DEALING WITH THE HOME-RUN HITTER

When you're up against a slugger, don't despair. The threat of sudden annihilation is ever present, but I think there are also advantages on the side of the pitcher facing a man who's trying to park one.

Sandy Koufax had a theory about the importance of retiring the eighth man in the line-up for the third out. Then, he said, you have the pitcher leading off. If you can put them down one-two-three, then in the following inning you'll have the third man in the lineup leading off. He's usually the best man on the club both for averages and distance, and it figures that the best hitter coming up with nobody on would be trying for a home run. What's so good about that, then? Well, home-run hitters just seem to strike out more than the average hitter, and if they have this tendency, they're obviously going to have less chance of getting a hit. (The same slugger at bat with a man on base will try to make contact, and then his chances of getting a hit will be higher.)

Obviously, you should try to stay out of the home-run hitter's power zone. That zone is easy to know in your own league, but it's quite a different story in interleague play. You may know someone is a fast-ball hitter, but does he like it over the heart of the plate or inside? Before the 1970 World Series, for example, they warned us it was impossible to get the fast ball past Lee May—and it just about was. We learned if you threw the fast ball up and away, he'd hit singles; if you threw it inside, he'd hit home runs. But up and in, you could get him out.

Against a hitter of the caliber of Johnny Bench, you simply want to make sure that if he's going to hit a home run, he's going to have to do it off a super pitch—a breaking ball out of his power zone.

In a situation where I'm facing a home-run hitter whose team is trailing 1–0, I try very hard to keep it away from him because I know he's going to be trying to pull the ball. I'll probably throw him some breaking stuff, because I know he's going to be looking for a fast ball and trying to hit it out in front, so he'll be susceptible to a breaking pitch. A well-thrown curve ball can throw the hitter completely off balance, because he not only has to follow the curvature of the ball, he also has to adjust to the change of speed. In other words, if he's seen fast balls all day and his bat and stride are geared for one, it will take quite a bit of doing to hit a ball that's a second slower.

Sometimes you have to take chances with a power hitter, but as a rule you should never let the opposing team's best hitter beat you. In other words, in a crucial situation —say you've got a 1–0 lead and they've got a man on with Johnny Bench at bat—you obviously would pitch very cautiously to him. Better to let him hit a single, or even pitch so carefully that you walk him, than let him beat you with a home run. Sometimes you'll throw a fast ball to a contact hitter like Gates Brown, figuring that this guy can't possibly hit a home run, and then—choo! —he just smacks it out.

HOMERS AND WALKS

In 1973 I threw fourteen home-run balls in 296 innings, which isn't very many for that much pitching.

I've said I'd rather give up a home run than walk a batter. That's easily misunderstood. What I meant was that where you have, say, a 3–1 lead, and you walk a man in the ninth inning to allow the potential tying run to come to the plate, you probably would have been as well off if that lead-off man had a home run, because then you could concentrate entirely on retiring the next man.

As a rule, solo homers aren't bad; it's the two-run and three-run blasts that you want to avoid.

Being too intent on not walking somebody can lead to difficulty sometimes. Mickey Mantle was already past his prime when I came up to the American League, and I struck him out six times in a row. Then on the seventh at-bat I got behind him, 2–0. I didn't want to walk him with Roger Maris and Elston Howard due up next, so I threw him a fast ball right down the middle and he hit it off the third deck of Yankee Stadium. I don't think that ball has come down yet.

When you're walking relatively few men, your total of pitches thrown for home runs goes up because you're throwing the ball over the plate more.

HITTERS WHO GIVE YOU TROUBLE

You'll probably find there are hitters who constantly give you trouble who aren't particularly good hitters, and hitters you have a rather easy time with who are excellent hitters. It's hard to explain.

My biggest nemesis is Doug Griffin, the second baseman for the Red Sox. In his first two years, he got something like sixteen hits in thirty-two times at bat against me, and in 1973 I did a little better against him, but he always hit line drives. His average has been between .260

and .280 against the league, but close to .500 against me. It just seems as if he always knows what I'm throwing.

Gates Brown of Detroit, the league's number-one pinch hitter, has had a fabulous career against me. It's amazing, but it's true: he averages a home run a game off me! I made him a star. People suggest I walk him, but you don't like to walk a man in Detroit (or Boston) because there's always the danger the next guy will hit a *two*-run homer. So players like these have pretty good success against me.

HITTERS WHO DON'T GIVE YOU TROUBLE

As I've already mentioned, although Harmon Killebrew will hit some home runs because he swings so hard, I've been pretty successful against him. I used to get Frank Howard out really well by pitching him high and tight. Then his manager, Ted Williams, who had been possibly the greatest hitter of all time, suggested that Frank move off the plate. He did, and he hit one of my pitches 500 feet for a home run. And suddenly I was thinking, "Maybe I can't get him out that well any more."

I used to get Reggie Jackson out pretty well. In one playoff game in 1971, he hit two home runs to the opposite field, but I had thrown the ball where I wanted to (which is some consolation). It was just that he was better than I was on that particular day, and he earned his homers. They were hit on low pitches outside the plate and he just went with them. He's so strong he was able to hit them out.

A pitch up and in is the best against a Reggie Jackson, but again I want to emphasize that it's more important to throw what you do best. If I start Reggie off inside and miss the plate, I'm behind on the count, 1–0. So now I know he's going to guess fast ball, because he knows I don't want to go to 2–0. On the next pitch, then, with that hypothetical 1–0 count, I would probably throw low and away, although he likes the ball there. I usually pitch left-handers better away, so I would usually try to pitch away to Reggie—and most of the time get him out.

Each pitch to Jackson (or anyone else, for that matter) will depend on the situation. If that first toss to him had been a strike rather than a ball, I might have thrown the same pitch (up and in) again, figuring that if I miss with it, the count is only 1–1.

The whole complexion of a game can be changed by any one ball-and-strike count, which is why plate umpiring is so important to a pitcher. A strike called a ball changes the circumstances and, depending on how you're pitching that day, might dictate that you do something differently.

Getting back to how well you handle particular hitters . . . sometimes your performance against one will fluctuate from season to season. When Carl Yastrzemski was having very good hitting years, I used to get him out very well. Then the last few seasons, when his hitting wasn't as good as it had been, he hit me exceptionally well.

Reggie Smith was an example of a reverse situation. He used to hit me very well, whacking line drives right back at me, off my knees and thighs. But then suddenly, it turned around, and I was getting him out more.

There's no predictable pattern with any hitter.

TOUGH TEAMS

You'll probably run up against teams that are especially tough for you, although they aren't necessarily the best teams around.

Sometimes that has to do with the fact that what you throw best is what they hit best. For instance, if you're a fast-ball pitcher and you face a team of good fast-ball hitters, it can spell trouble for you. I used to think that young hitters were basically good fast-ball hitters, while the older players, the veterans, had learned to hit the breaking ball. But you can't really generalize.

Detroit is a tough park to pitch in because of the short fences and the all-green background that makes the ball stand out for the hitter. Yet McNally and Cuellar would eat up the Tigers' lineup of fast-ball hitters. It's not only because Dave and Mike have good breaking stuff, but because they're lefties and a lot of the better Tiger hitters are left handed.

LEFT VS. RIGHT

It's generally true that a pitcher has the advantage over the man who bats from the same side of the plate as he throws. In other words, all other things being equal, I, as a right-handed pitcher, should do better against a right-handed batter than I do against a left-handed batter.

There are several reasons. A left-handed batter facing a right-handed pitcher sees the ball very well. Because they're able to see the ball way out to the side during the pitcher's motion, left-handed hitters usually "kill" righty pitchers who throw three-quarters and sidearm. They don't see the ball quite as well if it's thrown overhand.

The right-handed batter doesn't see the ball as well

when it's served up by a right-handed hurler, so chalk up one advantage for the pitcher.

Another plus for the pitcher is the fact that a breaking ball thrown by a righty will break away from a right-handed batter. That's generally tougher to hit than a ball that breaks in on you.

By the way, I think left-handed pitchers are more effective against left-handed batters than righties are against right-handed batters. One reason is that it seems that, from the minor leagues on up, left-handed hitters don't get much experience hitting against left-handed pitchers because they're platooned. As a result, they're not used to having the ball break away from them. They get accustomed to it coming toward them, and when, in the majors, they suddenly bat against a left-hander whose breaking ball is away, it's an altogether different illusion, and the hitters don't do well.*

In contrast to the experience of left-handed hitters, right-handed hitters do get to see right-handed pitching much of the time, so they're not faced with any big adjustment in the majors. I'm not that great a hitter (although I did hit a big .230 one year), but I prefer hitting against right-hand pitching even though I'm a right-handed hitter.

The reason, primarily, is that even though I see the ball better on a lefty than on a righty, I never saw left-

*I think a lot of left-handers could be better hitters against left-handed throwers, and a lot of right-handed batters could be better hitters against righties, if they saw them more often. Now most major-league twenty-five-man rosters have enough good hitters from either side of the plate to platoon them without hurting the game. But I think it detracts from the reputation and value of potential .300 hitters like Ron Blomberg for him to play only against right-handers.

handed pitchers that well. Besides, a good pitcher has good control *away*. And just as I try to throw to left-handed hitters away, left-handed pitchers pitch me away. With a three-quarter delivery, the ball runs away from the hitter even more. When Dave McNally, a lefty with a fine breaking ball, faces a right-hander, he pitches sliders on the inside corner and throws running fast balls away from the batter. If you can do that, you can win twenty games every year. If you can't, and your breaking ball comes right over the middle of the plate and your fast ball doesn't jam the hitter, you're headed for trouble.

Basically, I try to pitch to both right-handed and left-handed hitters on the outer portion of the plate. My theory is that if I pitch them away, they won't pull the ball and thus won't hit as many home runs. Balls they hit will stay in the park.

Nevertheless, you should pitch to a righty differently than you do to a lefty.

To right-handed hitters, I throw a lot of sliders because that's a pitch that will break away from them. But obviously a slider that's low and away to a right-hander is low and *in* to a left-hander—and because most left-handed batters are naturally low-ball hitters, that slider is going directly to their power. The only place you can safely throw a slider to a lefty is low and away on the outside corner, but that's easier planned than done, because you're so used to throwing it on the opposite part of the plate. If you throw a low and inside pitch for a strike, a good left-handed hitter will probably belt a double down the line or a homer out of the park.

When you get ahead of the left-handed batter, you

might try a slider belt high and in, to move him off the plate, or to lure him into chasing a bad pitch. If he doesn't bite, though, it's a ball, but that's the chance you have to take.

I don't really mind pitching against left-handers. For one thing, I have a little bit of a change-up that goes away from them. At Yankee Stadium, where my opposition were all left-handed hitters, I found that if I got behind with my fast ball, the change-up was an excellent pitch. They'd think it was a fast ball and they'd lunge, with the result that I got a lot of easy outs.

Also, I can usually spot my fast ball on the outside part of the plate—but there are also days when the ball goes over the middle, and then the left-handers really give you a lot of trouble.

I have a good overhand curve ball that doesn't really come in that much, but rather goes down, and I throw left-handers a lot of slow curves. Surprising as it may seem, I have trouble throwing curve balls to right-handers because those hitters are in my view as I come through. My curve ball seems better to left-handed hitters, probably because I don't see the hitter that much; all I see is the catcher.

This is just one more piece of evidence showing you how much better off you are looking at the catcher when you pitch. Often, you'll throw curve balls to a right-handed hitter and the ball will stay inside because you've been throwing off his body instead of doing what you should—just looking at the catcher and more or less blocking out the batter. Admittedly, that's hard to do, but it's what you *should* do.

PITCHING AGAINST A SWITCH HITTER

Say there's a switch hitter due up with a man on first or a runner in scoring position. If I were the manager and had a choice of putting in either a right-handed or left-handed pitcher to face him, I'd probably put in the left-hander in order to encourage the switch hitter to bat righty. The reasons? For one thing, more right-hand hitters are double-play hitters. Also, if the right-handed batter should single on the ground to left field, the runner may hold up, not knowing whether the ball is going to go through or be fielded by the shortstop, whereas he's likely to be running on any ball to the right side.

THE DESIGNATED HITTER

The designated hitter rule, adopted by the American League, lets a team pick one man to pinch-hit for one player throughout the game, without the hitter ever having to play the field, and without requiring the player he hits for to·leave the game.

It's certainly a good rule for the fans, providing more interest in the game because more runs are being scored.

In addition, it's kept some ball players in baseball who would otherwise have been out of the sport, either because they were getting old, although their hitting was about as good as ever, or were good hitters but not very good fielders or runners.

The designated hitter rule has made the pitcher's job more difficult, because now he's facing nine real hitters instead of eight. Where once there were certain bunt situations with the pitcher up at bat, they're no longer "giving" you that out. And you no longer have an almost sure out when the ninth man in the batting order comes to bat, as you did when it was the pitcher—the average pitcher hits in the neighborhood of .100—an almost sure strike-out if you make good pitches.

But the designated hitter rule also has some advantages for the pitcher. Formerly, he would have been pinch-hit for and taken out of the game; now he gets to stay in the game longer. This is why I think we had twelve twenty-game winners in the American League, which has the rule, and only one in the National League, which doesn't have the rule.

Of course, you may stay in the game too long and thus hurt the ball club. For instance, you may be left in because you're an established starter, possibly your team's ace, and then you end up yielding that one extra run that defeats your club.

But overall it's definitely a good rule, and easy enough to get used to.

PITCHING IN A CLOSE GAME

There are some general tips to follow when pitching in a close game.

Probably the most important thing is to get the first batter out. That's a cardinal principle of pitching, mainly because if you get that first man out, you could conceivably load up the bases and still get out of the inning with a double-play ball. So concentrate particularly on that first batter every inning.

Not only with the first batter, but with *every* batter, try to stay ahead of the count. When you're ahead, hitters seem to be a little more defensive and try just to make contact, thereby reducing the chances of home runs. Conversely, if you're behind the hitter, you have to come across with the pitch and he can hit it out of the park.

In a close ball game every pitch has meaning, so concentrate more than you would with a big lead.

It's much harder for a pitcher with a team that doesn't score many runs than one who pitches for a high-scoring club, not only in terms of mental strain but physical fatigue. Being constantly involved in one-run games, where you know one mistake can cost the ball game, is wearing.

Part of this concentration is always knowing what you're going to do whether the ball is hit to you, to one of your outfielders, or one of your infielders. In any game, close or not, you should be prepared for every situation. In close games it's most important.

PITCHING WITH A BIG LEAD

Pitching with a big lead is pleasant, but not without danger. When you've got a big lead, your concentration starts to wander, and soon the big lead becomes a small lead or even a deficit.

When your team is far ahead, basically you've got to pitch the same way as you would if the score were close. It's hard to get yourself to do that, but this element is really what separates a good pitcher from the so-so pitcher. The good pitcher will have control of all his faculties and be able to make himself concentrate by saying to himself something on the order of "This is a very important hitter," as if he had only a one-run lead.

Of course, there are some luxuries that a big lead affords you. In a one-run game you can't give in to a hitter and throw the ball down the middle when you get behind. But with a big lead you don't have to be so cautious that you walk a man. Sometimes with a 3–2 or 2–2 count, instead of trying to strike the batter out, you just make sure you throw a strike. You risk the possibility that the batter might get an extra-base hit, but you've also given your team a shot at making a play in the field.

PITCHING WHEN YOUR TEAM IS FAR BEHIND
When you find yourself pitching in ball games in which your team is far behind, you'll have to fight the tendency to give up. Sure, it's frustrating to be behind early in the game, but that doesn't mean it's hopeless.

In the 1970 World Series I gave up three runs in the first two innings to Cincinnati, and was wondering how I could possibly win. My team hadn't made up that much of a deficit for me all season, and wasn't likely to do it now. Besides, I figured, I'd have to shut out the Reds the rest of the way.

Still, I didn't give up. I tried to determine what I'd been doing wrong that had resulted in their runs. I came to the conclusion that one reason was a hanging curve ball to Lee May; the other, that my pitches in general hadn't been very good.

I bore down and did shut the Reds out for the next seven innings, while my teammates eventually came up with enough runs to take the game, 4–3.

Defense

PITCHING IS only one part of your defensive responsibilities. You're part of the infield, and as such you've got to be prepared to catch batted balls and throw to bases, cover bases, tag runners out, back up your teammates, participate in rundowns—in short, do just about everything any infielder does. As a matter of fact, you've got some extra defensive duties. For instance, when there's a runner on base it's your job to hold him where he is, or help try to pick him off, if possible. But first things first. . .

COORDINATING PITCHING AND DEFENSIVE ALIGNMENT

It's essential that the way you intend to pitch to a batter is coordinated with where your fielders position themselves to play him. That's one of the things we take up at clubhouse meetings.

Because a pitcher knows where he's going to pitch somebody, he should be the one—even more than the catcher—to dictate where the fielders play. Let's say you're going to pitch inside to a right-handed pull hitter. You know he's going to try to pull the ball, so you have to defense him around to left; you're certainly not going to play him toward right field. (It's easier to defense against a pull hitter than a player who sprays the ball to all fields.)

In the 1966 World Series, we decided that if we were going to beat the Dodgers, we had to keep Maury Wills off base. Maury was primarily a fast-ball hitter, but because he hit the ball so well to the left side of the infield and could run so fast, we decided we had to overshift him to the left and throw him fast balls to make him hit in that direction. With the whole infield and outfield shifted to left, we weren't going to throw him a slow breaking ball that he could loop to right field for a triple. I think the reason we did so well in that Series was that Grabowski, McNally, Bunker, and I made the pitches to Maury that we had to. We pitched him one way and our fielders played him accordingly, and we were successful. With our fielders overshifted, as they were, he could have really hurt us if we'd made a mental mistake and thrown him a slow curve ball or something similar. And he wouldn't even have had to hit the ball hard to damage us.

Of course, this kind of planning doesn't always work 100 percent, primarily because you can't always make your pitches go exactly where you want them to.

The late Roberto Clemente was the kind of batter who hit the ball as well to left field as to right. They said you had to pitch him inside and outside because he was

179

such a good hitter. We couldn't do either. We never got the ball consistently inside or consistently outside, so he went to town on us. He hit one home run to left field to beat us; he hit another homer off me to right field, and he got thirteen other base hits in that seven-game Series.

Because we couldn't do what we were supposed to do in our pitching, our fielders couldn't defense him adequately. It illustrates again why a hitter who is capable of going to all fields, hitting all over the park, is a lot tougher to pitch to and defense against, because you don't know where he's likely to hit the ball. This is the reason Ted Williams and the things he did were so remarkable. They'd stack the defense against him and yet he'd still hit the ball by them.

YOUR DEFENSIVE ASSIGNMENTS

After you've coordinated your pitching with your fielders, you have to concern yourself with your own defensive assignments.

BEING READY TO FIELD
You should release your pitch in such a way that you're ready to handle a ball hit right at you, or to your right or left—whether it's a line drive, chopper, or ground ball. Your glove should be up, your weight on the balls of your feet, and your eyes on the ball.

HANDLING LINE DRIVES
If a line drive is smacked back at you, the first thing to do is to protect yourself, especially from being hit in the face.

To do this, you've got to get your glove up fast. In 1973 Jon Matlack of the Mets was seriously injured near the eye on a line drive back at him, when he didn't get his glove up soon enough to protect his forehead. Sometimes, of course, the ball is hit too hard to do much but duck.

If you have a shot at spearing the line drive, try to use two hands. Sometimes, although you won't catch it, you'll be able to knock the ball down and retrieve it in time to retire the batter. Don't give up on a ball you've knocked down. Often, you'll be able to deflect the ball in such a way that your shortstop or second baseman can throw the man out at first. Even if it should go for a hit, though, the important thing is to avoid serious injury.

BOUNDING BALLS

When the batter bounces one back at you, make sure you watch the ball all the way into your glove. If it's hard hit, treat it as you would a line drive. At least try to deflect it so you can keep the ball in the infield and hold the batter to one base. With luck it can be turned into a force-out or a play at first.

POP FLIES

Pop flies are best handled by someone in the infield other than the pitcher. The others are more experienced at catching them. You can do your part by getting out of the way, and perhaps yelling or signaling to the man who has the best chance at catching it.

COMMUNICATING—ESPECIALLY ON BUNTS

Particularly on a bunt, one of the most important things a pitcher must remember to do is let his first or third baseman know he's going to field the ball—unless and until he's called off.

Just yell something like "I have it" or "I'll take it" or "I'll get it," to get your message across. And if one player thinks a teammate is in better position to handle a ball, he'll shout, "*You* take it" or "*You* get it."

When a ball is bunted you should go after it, until the first baseman, third baseman, or catcher calls you off it. On a bunt down the third-base line, for instance, the third baseman will probably have a better angle and thus the momentum going toward first base, so he'll make the play.

But often it's the pitcher who's in the best position to handle a bunt.

The biggest consideration in a bunt situation is that you get at least one out, preferably the lead runner, of course. You don't want to make a hurried throw or throw to the wrong base and thereby open the floodgates to a big inning by failing to get even one out. So, especially in a close game, try to get the lead runner if possible but, above all, retire at least one of the men. Normally, a good catcher will tell you what base to throw to, since he has a view of the whole situation before him.

With a man on first in a bunting situation, be ready to go after a bunt hit down either foul line. With runners on first and second, the best thing to do is pitch the ball and 'run immediately to the third-base line, because the hitter will be trying to avoid a force at third base and thus will likely aim the bunt that way to bring the third baseman in. It's very rare, unless the ball is bunted straight back at you, that you're able to get a force; you usually have to be content with getting the bunter at first. But sometimes you're lucky—and some players will tell you they'd rather be lucky than good.

THROWING TO BASES

The main point in throwing to a base is that you've got to sight either the man or the base you're throwing to. Secondly, you've got to throw when you're well balanced, with your left shoulder (if you're a righty) facing your target. The same theory applies here as in pitching: you've got to drive properly, with your shoulder aiming right at the target, and you have to step so that your weight is transferred smoothly from back foot to front.

For instance, when I'm fielding a bunt down the first-base line, I try to come over and pick the ball up with the weight on my left foot. Then I take sort of a crow hop and step forward, with my weight on my right foot and my left foot toward the base. On a bunt down the third-base line, I come over with the weight on my right foot, pick the ball up, crow hop, then throw with my right foot planted and my left foot again toward first base.

A right-hander should wheel to his left (counterclockwise) to make the throw to first, whether he's fielded the ball on the first- or third-base line.

Timing Your Throw. When there's a runner on first and the ball is bunted, chances are that the first baseman (and third baseman) will be charging in, so the second baseman will be covering first. If you field the bunt, you should wait if possible until he's just about arrived, then throw the ball right to the bag. A good second baseman will normally be at the bag in plenty of time because he anticipated the bunt. On what shapes up as a very close play, you have to lead him—that is, throw to the base before he gets there. In this situation, you anticipate how long it will take the second baseman to arrive at the bag, and then you time your throw so that the ball and he get there together.

It's a very dangerous throw, because the runner may be arriving at the same time. So don't throw the ball across the bag, but to its inside edge, so the infielder can catch it on the infield side.

Keeping Your Hands Together. You have to make your throw when you're on balance or risk a bad throw. And you have to pick up the runner. But probably the most important point to remember is that when you pick up the ball, keep your hands together. Don't let your arm drag behind your body, because if you do this and start to throw, you may realize that the second baseman isn't quite there yet. Then you'll have to sort of "double clutch" —get your arm back into proper throwing position and lose precious time that could cost you the putout.

But if you hold your hands together and just swing your arm into the throwing motion, you're on balance and can make a much quicker throw.

Throwing for a Force. On a bunt or a ground ball when there might be a chance for a force—or even a double play—and you're planning on throwing to second base, you've got to know which fielder, the shortstop or the second baseman, is going to be covering. This should be determined by prearranged signal before you pitch the ball. Generally, on right-handed pull hitters the second baseman covers (since a righty pull hitter will probably hit toward shortstop); on left-handed pull hitters the shortstop covers (since lefties are likely to hit toward the second baseman).

BACKING UP A PLAY

We don't have any relays from the outfield that the pitcher is expected to cut off, since all relays into the infield are covered by the first or third baseman. But of course the pitcher is expected to back up teammates at bases automatically.

On a single, for example, you should back up the infielder to whom the ball is going to be thrown. Let's say there was a man on first and a single is hit to right. You should run directly behind third base to back up there.

If there's a runner on first and the batter hits a probable double, on which you know the runner is surely going to third and might try to make it home, position yourself halfway between third and the plate. This affords you a good angle and enough leeway to cover third if the ball goes there, or home, if that's where the throw is directed.

Certain situations pose no problems. If there's a man on second and the batter hits a single, you go right behind home plate, and stand deep enough behind the catcher so if it's a high throw you'll be able to retrieve it.

There are all sorts of situations, and usually your action is dictated by your own good logic. If the shortstop and second baseman are out after a ball, and the base they normally cover is uncovered, then you know you have to cover it. When, with a man on second, a pop fly is hit down the left-field line and the third baseman and shortstop both go out for it, you have to cover third. When, with a man on first, the batter hits a pop that might drop into short center field, you should cover second base. And you'd also cover second base on a pop fly down the right-field line, whether or not there's a runner on base.

Covering First.   On any ball hit to the right side of the infield, toward the first or second baseman, it should be an automatic reflex for you to break immediately to first base. If the first baseman handles the ball, it's your job to cover first. Similarly, on any slow-hit ball to the first baseman, it's the pitcher's job to cover. And you want to be heading toward first on a pop-up in foul territory or fair in the vicinity of first base.

A straight line may be the shortest distance between two points, but when you're going to cover first, you should run to a point about halfway or two-thirds of the way down the first-base line, then run directly parallel with the base line to the bag. As you run toward the base, you should face the man fielding the ball. You should time your speed and be sufficiently well balanced to be able to arrive at the bag, stop, and then make your stretch to take the throw. You don't want to be running at full speed, because if the throw is a little bit off to the right or left, you'll have to lunge for the ball and not be able to come back to the bag.

It goes without saying that you've got to keep your eye on the ball all the way, especially because handling a throw and covering a base is something that is foreign to you.

TAGGING THE RUNNER
When you're covering a base and the runner is sliding into

186

you, do your best to avoid being spiked on your pitching hand—or anywhere else, for that matter.

Because tagging someone is pretty foreign to a pitcher, it's important that you watch the ball all the way so you can make sure you catch it before you make the tag. Grasp the ball firmly in your glove and make a sweeping motion, so the runner slides into the tag. Make sure you touch him, but don't leave your hand and glove there any longer than necessary, because the runner may either kick the ball out or spike you.

When you're trying to tag a runner who's not sliding, try to tag him low. You should normally have the ball in your glove, held there by your bare hand so that the ball won't come out of the glove on impact. A good idea is to keep your glove away from the front of the runner, so you avoid being jarred. Tag him on the side, but make sure you tag him. You should be in sort of a crouch position in case he does slide. You know he's not going to jump over you; the only thing he can try to do is slide under you. So you should be in a position to more or less go down to make the tag.

RUNDOWN PLAYS

Pitchers have a role to play in rundowns.

If a runner is caught between first and second, you go behind first. If there's a rundown between third and home, you usually go behind home, while if it's between second and third, you go behind third, because normally the center fielder will be coming in to help out near second base. Again, it's essentially a matter of common sense: you go to the base that's unoccupied or the area that needs help.

Of paramount importance is making the smallest number of throws possible. The fewer the throws, the better chance of getting the man out. And don't stay in the base line, because if you do and the runner charges into you, you'll be called for interference and the runner declared safe at the base farther along. When you make your rundown, keep the ball at shoulder level, ready to release it at all times. This way, the runner won't know when you're going to throw, and you won't waste any time when you do. Also, throw the ball at shoulder level, because then you can throw the ball to your teammate over the runner's head, if necessary.

PICK-OFF PLAYS

If you can pick a runner off base, you've turned a potential run into an out. Your pick-off technique is worth working on.

Runner on First. When you're trying to pick a man off first base, the basic maneuver is to throw over to first base, again and again if necessary. With Horace Clark on first, I've thrown over as many as seven times in vain, then picked him off on my eighth try. Throwing over not only picks off a player occasionally, it makes the runner stay closer to the bag, which sometimes keeps him from taking an extra base on a subsequent hit, or prevents a steal, or helps you get a force-out or double play.

The primary thing you want to do to a runner on first is minimize his lead. Yet there are some players—Tommy Harper is one—who take tremendous leads and yet avoid being picked off because they're such good base runners, and they know when you're coming over there with a throw.

In this connection left-handed pitchers have an advantage. In their normal stretch motion, they're looking at the runner on first base so, consequently, they know exactly when to throw, and the runner has very little indication of when the throw is coming. But whether you're a right-handed or left-handed pitcher, there's an advantage to facing a right-handed batter with a man on first, because righty hitters are more likely to hit into a double play. For one thing, they're farther from first base than left-handers are. In addition, they're likely to hit the ball to the shortstop, who's probably the best fielder on the club, or to the third baseman, who's likely to be a better fielder than the first baseman.

A second objective the pitcher should have with a runner on first is to keep him flat-footed when he gets his jump or gets ready to attempt a steal. You don't want him to have a running jump, because it will give him momentum toward second base and make it that much easier for him to steal the base.

A pick-off play at first can also originate with the catcher, who either calls for a pitchout and rifles the ball to first, or simply throws down after catching a normal pitch.

Runner on Second. When there's a runner on second base, you should see to it that he's going back toward second base as you make your pitching move toward home. This requires the assistance of your second baseman and shortstop, who keep ducking in behind the runner, ready to take a pick-off throw at second.

This also helps prevent the runner from taking too big a lead, an important defensive aim, because the easiest base to steal is third. A runner on first has the first baseman holding the bag against him, but a runner at second doesn't have the problem because the shortstop and second baseman have to play in fielding position.

So it's important to keep that runner close to second. Of course, the second baseman and shortstop shouldn't work so hard at it that they're out of position when the pitch is delivered.

There are various ways you can work a pick-off play at second.

One is what we call a "daylight play," which is essentially just visual. When the shortstop gets between the runner and second base, you wheel and throw—and hope. You've got to be careful on this play, or any other pick-off attempt for that matter, that you don't throw the ball away into the outfield.

A more commonly used play to second is the "count." You come into your stretch, look toward second, turn toward home and count, "One thousand one, one thousand two, one thousand three." At this point, usually the second baseman or sometimes the shortstop (who is also counting) breaks for the bag and you turn around and throw the ball.* A word of caution: You don't *have* to throw in this situation. It's silly for a pitcher to make any throw he doesn't have to make, so if the runner is going to beat the infielder back to the bag, don't throw the ball. At best it will be a wasted throw; at worst, an error that allows the runner to advance.

---

*Who covers the base on a pick-off will depend on such factors as whether the hitter is right-handed or left-handed. If he's likely to hit to shortstop, the second baseman will cover.

Runner on Third. Tom Seaver says he hasn't moved to third base to pick off a runner in seven years. The odds of picking someone off third aren't good enough, he feels, compared to the odds of heaving the ball into left field. I agree. Occasionally, though, you will find an aggressive runner and a pick-off try will be necessary.

Signs and Countersigns. On the "count" pick-off play and some other specials, all the fielders involved have to know it's coming, so you've got to signal one another.

Usually the shortstop or second baseman will give the catcher the sign for a pick-off play and he'll flash it to you. (Occasionally, they'll give it to you directly.) Then you let them know that you've read the signal. On the counting play, for instance, I rub my glove down my left leg to let the catcher know that I'm aware. When I throw to second, I turn to my left, counterclockwise.

One play the Orioles use has the catcher give the pick-off sign. He'll go to his mask, then open his fist. Opening it once means the first baseman takes the throw; twice, the second baseman; three times, the shortstop; and four, the third baseman. We work on this in spring training to sharpen our timing and coordinate our moves. It works this way:

You go into your stretch, come down to the set position —your hands at the waist. You look at first or second base, depending on where the runner is located. (Second is the base to look at if there are runners on both first and second.) Then you turn and look at the catcher, who has a closed fist. When he opens his hand, you turn and throw to the infielder he's designated.

On that particular play, I once picked off Carl Ya-

To hold a runner close to the base or to attempt a pick-off play, use a stretch motion. Take the sign (A), go into your stretch (B). Come down to the set position (C), your hands at your waist (D). Look at first base or second, depending on where the runner is. Then either throw to the base— the catcher may be signaling for a pick-off—or kick and drive toward the plate (E).

strzemski to get us out of a big inning early in the game, which was played in Boston. Unfortunately, all it did was prolong our losing until the ninth inning, when Carl doubled off the left-field wall and scored the winning run.

The Pick-off Play and the Balk.   One danger confronting a pitcher when he tries to pick off a runner is a possible balk. A balk is a violation that allows the runner or runners to advance a base. There are specific rules concerning what a pitcher may or may not do once his foot makes contact with the pitching rubber. But often the question of whether a pitcher has balked is not clear-cut, and it comes down to an umpire's judgment.

If you start delivering the ball to the batter and then switch directions and fire to a base instead, you'll be called for a balk. If you're a right-hander about to throw to first, you've got to wheel around and step in the direction of the base. Once you've done that, you *must* throw there, or be charged with a balk. With a man on second or third, though, you can turn around without necessarily making the throw. And you don't have to take your foot off the rubber to make the throw. For instance, to go to third you can come to your stretch and lift your front foot as if you're going to pitch, and then step toward third base.

What you can't do is move your left leg behind the rubber. If you do, you have to throw home; otherwise, you can go right to third base. The same thing applies to a left-handed pitcher and first base. Your kicking leg can't go behind the rubber if you're going to throw legally over to the base.

Left-handers with excellent pitching motions, such as

Dave McNally, now an Expo, and Bill Lee of Boston, keep the left leg where they can legally go either way.

There are other ways of balking, too. Once you start your windup, you have to continue it, unless you step off the rubber and, in a continuous motion, throw to the base. Once you start moving your hands up, you have to continue or step off, which isn't very difficult once you've trained yourself to do it.

When a runner breaks for home, the best thing to do is throw the ball high and tight. This makes it more difficult for the batter to bunt, and he gets out of the way.

I think balks are caused by difficulties in concentration. You've got to know where the runners are, and you have to consider in advance what the base runner might do. Is he going to make a feint toward second, or what? You also have to determine what the hitter might do with the runner on. A pitcher rarely balks if he's mechanically sound, if he knows what to do and has practiced what he has to do.

That's no guarantee, though. I used to wind up with a runner on third, a dangerous tactic because a good base runner can almost score while you take your normal windup.

In a televised "Game of the Week" against Oakland, I found out how dangerous it is. Campaneris was on third, and as I went into my windup, I saw him break for the plate. I stepped off the rubber and in the same motion took the ball out of my glove and threw to third. The umpire didn't realize what was happening, and called a balk. He didn't realize I was moving my hands toward each other so that I could get the ball for the throw to third. He said I'd started my hands in my upward motion over my head. (By the way, the reason I didn't have my pitching hand on the ball in the glove, as I usually do, is that with a man on third it's hard to take your hand out without stepping off the rubber.)

So it's a fine line. Ever since that incident, I've gone into a stretch with a man on third.

In spring training in 1974, an experiment was introduced in which lines were drawn in a 45-degree-angle V from the pitching rubber, to help umpires rule when a balk has been committed. If the pitcher's front foot swings beyond one of the lines (toward home) he must deliver the pitch; if he throws to first instead, he's guilty of a balk.

The rule stands to hurt left-handed pitchers most, since, as they naturally face the bag, they're much more apt to use a deceptive move toward first base from a stretch than are right-handers, whose backs are to first.

The Psychology
of Pitching

I DON'T BELIEVE there's another position in base-ball in which mind and emotions play such an important role as they do with pitching. All the natural talent in the world isn't enough unless you know what to do with it, and unless you can put your feelings to work positively for you.

FRAME OF MIND

Your frame of mind when you pitch is of great significance, because it will determine how much you're able to do with your ability on a given occasion. If you think you're tired, you're going to be tired; if you don't think you can get a hitter out, you're probably not going to, whereas if you think you *can* get him out, most of the time you will.

Many hitters a pitcher faces are quite awesome, and

when any hitter, awesome or not, starts hitting you with regularity, you develop the attitude that you can't get him out. As a result, you become a defensive pitcher and you don't throw the ball as well or as hard as you normally would. Consequently, what you started to suspect—that you can't get him out—becomes a reality.

SELF-CONFIDENCE

You have to believe in yourself and what you can do.

For example, I've generally felt that I can get most hitters out, although I'm realistic enough to know that hitters are going to get their hits. But even if a batter gets a home run off me, I'll tell myself that the reason he hit it was that I made a bad pitch or didn't throw the ball as well as I'm capable of doing. And if it was a fast ball he hit, I'll come right back the next time he's up and throw him a fast ball, knowing that if I throw it well and in the proper place, I'll probably get him out.

This doesn't mean you don't learn from what happened. If the home run he hit was off a good pitch, then you've probably got to change what you throw him. But if he hit the homer on a pitch you didn't throw well, you know you can get him with a good pitch of the same variety.

Confidence played a big part in my success in the first game of the 1973 playoffs against the A's, when I pitched five scoreless innings without very good stuff, but with the help of good pitches I made with my breaking ball. When you know you can do things on the mound, it makes it easier to pitch. But when there is a little doubt in your mind, when you're not really sure you can do what you want to do, you're going to be held back. Self-doubt makes it much more difficult to pitch well.

NERVOUSNESS

I had always thought that the more money I made in base-ball and the more success I had, the less nervous I'd be before I took the mound, but it doesn't work that way. The more you progress, the more people expect of you, so there's more pressure on you.

Pregame apprehension is normal, and it can even be helpful if you channel it properly. All great actors say they feel "butterflies" in the stomach before they go on stage, and somehow that anxiety and the flow of adrenaline it stimulates help them with their performance.

It should work the same way with pitching. As soon as you go out and perform and get involved in what you're doing, you're too busy to remember that you're nervous. I've found my nervousness ends once the game begins. Even in great pressure situations, even where you have a 3–2 count on the batter with the bases loaded, if you're prepared for it, if you've mastered the basics and prac-ticed them, you should have your nerves under control.

I have to admit that nervous apprehension used to make me tired, and it bothered me. Then one year I asked myself: "Why should you be tired? Your arm feels all right and your legs are in great shape." Somehow that pep talk helped me over the feeling of nervousness. It's essen-tially a matter of mental preparation.

No doubt, batters are nervous, too—especially those who know you usually get them out—but they don't show it very much.

If anything, batters contribute to the pitcher's nervous-ness. When I was in the Babe Ruth League, we were playing the first game of the regionals in Tooele, Utah, against Southern California. The other team had all huge kids on it, and I can still remember the first one getting up to bat, with a big grin on his face. That shook me so much I walked the first eight batters. Because I was the best pitcher on the team, the manager wouldn't take me out. It was amazing how I just walked one batter after another, just because of that first kid and his grin.

BELIEF IN SUPERSTITIONS

It's foolish to depend on superstition to help you in your pitching. Just because I kept wearing a pair of faded, hand-me-down orange socks as long as I kept winning in 1973 doesn't make me superstitious. And neither does the Watergate bug I kept with me everywhere I went. People think it's crazy to put stock in things like that, but I'd had good luck since I was given that coin (which featured a large beetle wearing headphones connected to a recorder). Before a game against Boston, I realized I'd forgotten it and I panicked, but two minutes before I began warming up, my wife, Susie, brought it to me in a taxicab. I won the game.

PRESSURE

Certain games put more pressure on a pitcher than others, and some hurlers get reputations for being able, or unable, to win the "big ones."

The reputation isn't always deserved. For example, they speak of Vida Blue's inability to win them,* but

---

*Vida Blue lost fourteen post-season games in a row until he faced me in that third playoff game in 1974. I held Oakland to four hits and one run, but he held the Orioles scoreless on two singles. He proved he *could* win a big one.

very often it's a matter of his team's inability to produce runs for him, as when we beat him, 6–0, in the 1973 play-off opener.

I've been fortunate enough to win most of the so-called big games—the playoffs and Series games—I've pitched over the years. But while I've pitched in important contests, I feel I haven't had to pitch in very many high-pressure ones. I say this, even though in three different playoffs I won the third game of the best-of-five series. Each time, though, we were already up 2–0 in games, and I always figured that if we didn't win the playoffs in the game I pitched, we'd win it in the next game or the one after that. In those third games, I felt a lot less pressure than the man who pitched the first or second game.

I did pitch a first game in the 1973 playoffs, and it turned out to be probably the best game I ever pitched. I had the best fast ball I've ever had. In fact, the nail on my middle finger was bruised because I'd been trying to throw as hard as I possibly could.

Pressure is a matter of degree. I pitched the pennant clincher in 1966, but we were ten games up, so it was a lot different from going down to the last day of the season tied, and then pitching in the deciding game, the way Tiant did against Joe Coleman in 1972, with Tiant losing something like 2–1. *That's* a pressure game. In those days there were no divisional playoffs, and once you clinched a pennant, you knew you were going to the World Series. So when I won the pennant clincher in the old Kansas City ball park, I was overwhelmed by the awesome idea that I was going to be in the World Series. I was already getting nervous.

As nervous as I was about the prospect, however, I was

very pleased to draw the assignment for the second game, which we won after Willie Davis of the Dodgers made three errors that allowed us to score six runs.

One game in my career that has to qualify as a pressure cooker was the sixth game of the 1971 World Series against the Pirates. We were down three games to two, and early in this game I gave up two runs to Pittsburgh. But I shut them out for seven innings, and we came back to win the game on a bad hop in the tenth inning—and the Series was tied.

Nowadays, it seems, the real pressure games are the ones that get you into the World Series, rather than the Series games themselves.

Pressure or not, you have to just go out and do the best you can. As a major-league starter you'll pitch about forty times a year. If you know you've done the best job possible and you lose, you have to content yourself with the knowledge that you're going to have another chance. Of course, there will be times, as in the fourth or fifth game of a playoff, when there's no tomorrow. In 1973, when we were down two games to one in the playoffs against Oakland, we were joking that there would be no pressure tomorrow. The only question was whether we were going to get another day's meal money or go back home.

PSYCHING OUT THE HITTERS

Psychology can be a valuable ally of a pitcher. Since it's such a big part of the game, some pitchers will try to psych out a hitter, to work on his mind and possibly develop an emotional edge—an edge that's translated into strikes and weak swings and outs.

Some, capitalizing on a batter's natural fear of wildness, will deliberately throw the first pitch over the batter's head to the backstop, or throw a ball well inside. It's true that the batter's fear is a tremendous aid to the pitcher. I've hit very few batters in my career, but I'm aware that just the fact that a hitter knows you can be wild will affect the way he stands at the plate.

One of the things I often do to shake a batter up is to shake off signs. Say the catcher calls for a fast ball. I'll shake him off, and keep shaking him off until he calls for a fast ball again. Constant shaking off of signs is bound to make the hitter edgy. It's especially effective when the count is such—say 2–2—that a batter can be almost positive I'll throw a fast ball. My shaking my head ruins his train of thought and, unable to figure out what I'm thinking, he'll probably step out of the box.

In spring training I try to set up hitters for the season. I don't normally throw curve balls on a 3–2 count, but once or twice a game in training, I will throw one, and the hitter will be looking for it the rest of the year. It's a matter of doing something you don't normally do so it preys on his mind and he has to look for the unusual in the future.

I may do the same thing early in a game during the season—throw a curve ball with a 3–2 count, even though it's not a percentage pitch. I do it because I know if I get it over it's going to scramble his mind.

You can do things in your windup to disturb a hitter. For instance, when you're pitching from the stretch, maybe hold the ball a little longer than usual so the hitter tenses up from holding the bat up too long. Also, you can double pump—bring your arms up and down twice instead of once—to deceive the batter or get him off balance. The trouble with this is that you may disturb your own rhythm as well as the batter's. So unless you're really experienced and know what you're doing, you're better off sticking with your normal delivery.

Psyching works both ways, of course. When Eddie Watt pitches against a hitter who takes a lot of time, he'll step off the rubber every time the hitter finally gets set. I can remember pitching a particular opening day one year in Baltimore. I eventually won the game, 7–1, but late in the game my arm was getting tired. Tony Oliva, who probably takes more time getting set at the plate than anyone except Carlton Fisk, was infuriating me. Every time I'd get set to pitch to him, Tony would take about sixty seconds to dig in. He got me so angry I tried to throw the ball harder, with the result that my arm got loose again and I finished the game.

CONTROLLING YOUR EMOTIONS

It's important to learn to control your emotions, at least outwardly. I believe that a cool exterior, one that doesn't let either your teammates, your opponents, or the umpire know how you feel, adds up to a psychological advantage for you.

I may be churning inside, but I try not to show it. Luckily, I haven't had too difficult a time controlling my emotions, although in the heat of battle I sometimes get so competitively involved that my emotions do show.

But I can assure you I don't kick lockers or throw bats the way some guys do. I think when you do that kind of thing, you can only eventually injure yourself and hurt your ball club. There's certainly no real personal satisfaction in an outburst like that. When things go wrong, I try to sit down and analyze what I did wrong and correct it next time. Normally there's an explanation for just about everything you've done wrong.

Some pitchers get so frustrated at a batter who keeps getting hits off them that they'll throw at him. I feel when you have to throw at a hitter to intimidate him, maybe you should get out of pitching.

The hitter's ability against yours is a fundamental part of the game. One day you're going to win and one day you're going to lose. If you can say to yourself, "I lost but I gave my best," you can't ask for any more. If, however, you know inside that you did not give your best, then you should sit down and let it hurt you, and then promise yourself to do your best next chance you get.

Obviously you learn from your mistakes, and you should try to figure out why they happened so you can correct them. It's normal to replay games in your mind over and over again. Whether or not that constant replay is healthy depends on how you deal with it. If you can remember why you made a mistake so you don't repeat it, replaying the event can be helpful. But if it just makes you miserable, and you keep repeating the mistake, it's destructive.

Overthinking is an ever-present danger, especially when you're going bad. If you're doing well, you should never try to change yourself. Why tamper with success? When I'm pitching great, I just go out there and let the natural ability and mechanics of pitching do their work.

ARGUING WITH UMPIRES

It doesn't pay to argue with the umpires, although sometimes a call in a crucial situation is such a shock that you can't help yourself. But most of the umpires are very fair, and it's better to talk to them and discuss your gripe in a civil manner than blow up at them.

If you show your displeasure visibly, they might get upset because they think you're trying to show them up, but if you air your grievance in a polite manner, they're pretty respectful.

I don't argue very much, except when pitches down the middle that I think (or *know*) are strikes are called balls. I used to talk to the ump behind the plate about it when I came up to bat next time, but that chance vanished for me with the coming of the designated hitter.

Once I threw a fast ball right down the middle and the umpire, Bill Haller (Tom Haller's brother), called it a ball. I just couldn't believe it, and I did a double take. He just glared at me.

When I came up to bat next time, he said, "I don't care what you do. You can yell and scream as much as you like—the fans can't hear you yelling—but don't ever look at me like that, because the fans can see that." I'd always thought it was the other way around, that you could look angry but not yell, and I still think that's the case with almost every other umpire. Bill Haller chewed me out so much on that occasion that I missed the bunt sign.

Most umpires are pretty consistently correct in their calls. Contrary to what some players and managers think, the umpires are human, so they make some bad calls—and occasionally they try to even things up.

One All-Star Game, Ed Runge, who was the plate umpire, set an all-time record for All-Star Game strikeouts (nineteen). He'd give the pitchers the benefit of the doubt on the first two pitches, but then make them work for their third strikes. The hitters knew it, and so did the pitchers. That was one game when even pitchers not known for strikeouts got a few to their credit.

THE FANS

Fans can be a big help in boosting your confidence—or can help to undermine it—but if you're concentrating on your pitching you probably won't notice them very much.

In the 1973 playoffs, the warm-up mound had been taken away because the field was being readied for the football season, and I had to warm up in the bullpen. When I came to the mound, maybe because I'd had what was probably the best season of my career, I got a tremendous ovation from the fans. They say ball players are pretty much immune to that sort of thing, but it gave me chills.

During a game, we're generally not conscious of the fans. But when you're not pitching so well and your concentration is waning a little, you're aware of them, as I was in the third game of the 1969 World Series. I hadn't pitched in nine or ten days, and I really didn't know what I was doing out there on the mound. The Mets beat us, 5–0, thanks to a pair of outstanding outfield catches by Tommie Agee. I didn't pitch that badly—although Gary

Gentry, then of the Mets, got his only hit of the year, I think. Anyway, that was a day when I was well aware of the fans. But then, New York fans are a different breed of fans.

FEAR

A pitcher is sometimes confronted by two types of fear— he's afraid of being injured, and he's afraid of not doing well.

FEAR OF BEING HIT

You can't be afraid of being hit by a ball and still pitch successfully, any more than a batter can hope to hit well if he is frightened by pitches.

My most vivid fear is that I'll be hit by Frank Howard. I've always thought he's eventually going to hit a ball right through the middle at me. That hasn't happened, but in a 1973 playoff game against Oakland, I was almost wiped out by a shot that Reggie Jackson drilled down the middle.

Still and all, I don't really fear being hit by a batted ball—at least I don't think about it that much—because I have good reflexes and I usually am in a position to field the ball.

I've been hit at least twenty-five times by batted balls. It's inevitable. I throw thousands of pitches a year, and some are going to be hit through the box and get me on the leg or knee or elsewhere. The better positioned a pitcher is, the less likely he'll be hit—or hurt seriously.

There are no guarantees, of course. Jon Matlack got

hurt badly because a ball was hit back at him so quickly he couldn't get his glove up in time. But as frightening as an incident like that may be, you have to take the attitude that if it's going to happen, it's going to happen. It will hurt for a while, but that's part of the game.

So don't be afraid. Concentration—on where the ball is at all times, and on making sure you get into position to field it with your glove up—will help you overcome your fear. Dave McNally got hit in the left ear during a twi-night double-header against Cleveland in 1973. The next day, I can remember saying to myself, "I've really got to concentrate on following the ball all the way to the plate."

FEAR OF NOT DOING WELL

To forestall any fear of not doing well, just make sure to give your all-out best effort at all times. Then you'll have no cause for regret.

Certainly, you should be concerned about how well you perform and try accordingly to improve and refine your talents. But the most important thing is that you hustle and always give 100 percent.

DEALING WITH YOUR TEAMMATES

There will be times when a teammate kicks away a game you should have won, and you may be tempted to kick him. But remember, he wasn't *trying* to make an error. He feels bad enough without you getting on him.

My first year in a minor-league training camp, in Thomasville, Georgia, the shortstop made an error and the pitcher started berating him in front of all the other players. I couldn't help but wonder how that was going to affect the shortstop's playing effort. Probably he'd be afraid to make an error for fear the pitcher would yell at him again, so he would not go after hard chances, or else he might tense up and make errors on easy chances. Any time this happens, the pitcher is really hurting himself.

Mike Marshall gave his Montreal Expo teammates a tongue-lashing for their fielding. His comments were reported and he later apologized, but the damage was done. The Expos traded him to the Dodgers.

You have to take teammates' errors in stride. After all, you're part of the same team and, ideally, they're trying as hard as they can, just as you are.

If someone on the club is making errors because he isn't hustling, then it's the manager's place to say something, not yours. If it's happening all the time, then go talk to the manager about it.

You've got to remember you're part of a team, and that how well a pitcher does is really dependent on how well his team supports him. I know my success is due in great measure to the fact that we've had a great offense and defense. Certainly, I contribute by limiting the amount of times that batters get on base, but I know it's my teammates who make the plays in the field and score the runs. If they didn't score, I'd never win, no matter how well I pitched. And when they score three runs for me, if we're going to win, they have to keep the other team from scoring more than two. The point is, any help a pitcher gets from his teammates is something he should appreciate because they're going to make him a winning or losing pitcher.

LEARNING TO LOSE

Obviously, in professional sports winning is very important. At *any* level of play, of course, you want to win. But as an amateur you should take the attitude that other things are more important: playing with other youngsters and learning how to get along with them, and just being in sports and developing a sense of sportsmanship.

Losing is no disgrace if you've given your best. It's part of all sports, including professional competition. It's going to happen, and you have to accept the fact that you can't be successful every time out. You can't throw a tantrum every time you lose. Instead, content yourself with the fact that you're competing in a great sport, using physical and mental energy in competition against others your age who are trying *their* best. And determine that next time out you'll try just as hard, using all your natural ability coupled with all the skills you've learned and practiced. And you'll probably win.

JIM PALMER

Born in New York City, Jim Palmer was raised in Los Angeles and Scottsdale, Arizona. He won twenty or more games in four consecutive seasons, and was voted the Cy Young Award in 1973, a year in which he won twenty-two games and led all American League pitchers with a 2.40 earned run average. He has pitched a no-hitter against the Oakland A's, and won three World Series games.

Palmer presently resides in Timonium, Maryland, a Baltimore suburb. He and his wife, Susan, are the parents of two daughters, Jamie and Kelly.

JOEL H. COHEN

Joel H. Cohen is a free-lance writer who has written books with such stars as Tom Seaver, Bud Harrelson, Hank Aaron, Johnny Unitas, Kareem Jabbar and the Van Arsdale twins.